Landscapes

of the National Trust

Landscapes

of the National Trust

Stephen Daniels   Ben Cowell   Lucy Veale

National Trust

For Gail Lambourne and Charlotte Lloyd

First published in the United Kingdom in 2015 by
National Trust Books,
1 Gower Street, London W1CE 5HD
An imprint of Pavilion Books Group Ltd

ISBN 978 1 90789 281 3

A CIP catalogue record for this book is available from the British Library

Colour reproduction by COLOURDEPTH, UK
Printed by 1010 Printing International Ltd, China
Design: Lee-May Lim
Layout: Janis Utton
Project manager: Alison Moss

Printed on PREPS (Publishers' Responsible Environmental Paper Sourcing)
compliant paper.

This book can be ordered direct from the publisher at the website www.
pavilionbooks.com, or try your local bookshop. Also available from National
Trust shops and www.nationaltrustbooks.co.uk

Previous page | The quay on the Tamar River
on the Cotehele estate, near Saltash, Cornwall.

Right | The river, Pennard Pill, meanders its
way into Three Cliffs Bay in the Gower Peninsula,
South Wales.

Arts & Humanities Research Council

Landscape & Environment

Contents

Introduction Revealing Landscapes   6

Chapter 1 The Art of Landscape   16

Chapter 2 Ancient Places   62

Chapter 3 Homes and Gardens   110

Chapter 4 Lost in the Woods   162

Chapter 5 Open Country   210

Chapter 6 Shifting Shores   252

Acknowledgements   299
Bibliography   300
Credits   301
Index   302

Introduction

Revealing Landscapes

Landscapes matter. In town or country, on the coast or inland, landscapes are everywhere. They matter materially as physical places, and they matter culturally as sites of concern. They provide the setting for our daily lives and form an essential component of our sense of identity. Landscapes are lived in, worked on and moved through, as well as looked at. They inspire artists, writers, gardeners, architects, filmmakers, and others so much that landscapes are works of the imagination as well as physical sites, spaces and structures. Landscapes such as 'Constable Country' or 'The Garden of England' are places in the mind as well as places on the ground.

Why does landscape matter so much? The second half of the twentieth century saw a growing momentum for securing the protection of special landscapes. Immediately after the Second World War, National Parks were created as a gift to a nation newly freed from the constraints and impositions of life during wartime. International treaties such as the UNESCO World Heritage Convention offered recognition to landscape-scale areas, denoted for their special significance. The European Landscape Convention of 2000, meanwhile, posited a more open definition of 'landscape' as being any area shaped by the interactions of nature and humankind. This recognition that landscape surrounds us poses challenges for the idea of protection as it has come to be understood in relation to buildings and monuments. Change in the landscape can no more be resisted or stopped than can its historic character be erased overnight. Instead we must work with the grain of landscapes, by understanding their historical evolution and the cultural conventions that surround them.

Landscapes are never static but transform dramatically from season to season or from year to year, both naturally and as a result of human intervention. Landscapes change, though their constituent elements may do so on vastly different timescales. Trees inch upwards every year, coastlines crumble, rivers alter their course, and humankind leaves its own imprint on the landscape through buildings, roads and other developments. Wider economic, social and cultural contexts are critical to understanding the landscape. It is no coincidence that the first stirrings of movements to protect the landscape happened at a time of rapid industrialisation and urbanisation in the nineteenth century. Many of the upland landscapes that we admire today as pastoral idylls were, just a century or so ago, the sites of frenetic industrial activity: mining, smelting, burning. How we come to terms with landscape change, loss but also rebirth, is an issue that arises in many of the chapters in this book.

The landscape arts are changeful too, shaping the way we see our surroundings. The dominance of paintings of country house and prosperous farmland, and the poetry of mountain and moorland, gives way to photographers and writers keen to depict less picturesque scenes at the margins – declining towns and abandoned factories. But traditional arts do not give way entirely, still conditioning present views. While the paint on the canvas or the words on the page may not alter, the meaning they have will change over time, and the landscapes they portray will look different to readers and spectators from different periods and places. Constable's paintings and Wordsworth's poems are received differently now than at the time they were produced. 'Timeless scenes' are anything but. The meaning as well as appearance of landscapes on the ground will change too. What seems forbiddingly wild to one generation will seem appealingly natural to another; places that are disregarded at one time will be valued at another.

The National Trust was established in 1895 in order to protect landscapes for future generations. Its earliest aims were to see open spaces held in perpetuity for the nation. It was another half century before it was to gain a reputation for protecting country houses, and at various times in the last 120 years it has returned to the landscape as its core purpose. For example, the Neptune Coastline Campaign was launched in 1965 to raise funds for protecting coastal landscapes. Protection does not mean trying to hold back change; rather, it implies facing into the implications of change and taking a pragmatic approach to conserving and caring for places in the face of pressing developments. The task involves managing complex processes of natural and cultural change. This means being true to the abiding power and appeal of a landscape, while accepting that perceptions of places change no less than the places themselves, that landscapes will be valued in various ways.

Below | The Devil's Punch Bowl, a large natural amphitheatre in Surrey, is a designated Site of Special Scientific Interest and is maintained by the National Trust.

The book is a partnership, between the National Trust and the UK Arts and Humanities Research Council. Many of the projects which inspired this book were funded through the Council's Landscape and Environment programme. Some inform it directly through their subject matter, as case studies of places, others shape it more through their perspective. We are grateful to the many researchers, artists, writers and landscape explorers, past and present, who have helped shape this volume together. Like the best kind of landscape, this book is a meeting place as well as a vantage point, for displaying and discussing many views and visions.

The aim of this book is to reveal landscapes. It will throw new light on familiar scenes and iconic sites and also explore places off the beaten track. It will reveal what is hidden in plain sight as well as look at landscapes that are overlooked. It raises many questions. How much do we know about how different landscapes came into being? How have landscapes in the past been valued, and by whom? How were they lived in, shared, possessed, developed, argued over? What are the compelling stories to be told about such places and their people? How might the mentality as well as the materiality of historic landscapes be understood, conserved and communicated? How can landscapes today and in the future best adapt to the changing world in which we live?

More specifically, the book helps to demonstrate how the framing of a landscape is always a cultural act, requiring creativity and imagination. It is often personal, but never purely so, for as individuals we inherit a range of social attitudes to landscape, whether we are aware of these or not. Throughout the book, the focus returns to the

Left | Flowers adorn the doorway and front garden of a cottage in Lacock, Wiltshire. The fabric of this English village has been preserved over time, and it is noted for its picturesque streets, old workhouse, village tithe barn and timber-framed houses.

response of individuals to their landscapes while also considering the wider worlds in which their works were made.

This book provides new perspectives on a range of sites and scenes. It brings together the latest insights from researchers in the arts and humanities to illuminate the making and meaning of landscapes and bring them to life. The book draws on case studies from sites managed by the National Trust and others to illustrate the ways in which landscapes speak to a range and variety of concerns – about beauty, belonging, the past, access to nature and people's sense of place.

The book is structured thematically in six linked chapters that describe familiar kinds of landscape and ways of seeing them. Each chapter takes the form of a journey through landscapes, not as a conventional guided tour but as a trip through the imaginative as well as material world, through landscapes whose very power and enchantment stands at the intersection of cultural representation and physical reality. In each chapter there are two or three special photographic features which pick up on themes raised in the text and introduce additional National Trust properties and places.

The first chapter, The Art of Landscape, considers the interplay between actual landscape experience and its representation by creative artists, whether in the countryside, in the city or travelling abroad. For centuries visual artists and writers have adopted the landscape as their subject, in painting and sketching. This continues today in the work of contemporary artists who use landscape as a medium to explore questions of identity, memory and loss.

The second chapter, Ancient Places, explores the antiquity of landscapes, in particular those in which monuments and structures provide a principal focus of attention. Stonehenge is an especially iconic example, its stones forming the centrepiece of a wide and complex landscape of open grassland and prehistoric remains of different ages and meanings. At Hadrian's Wall, meanwhile, archaeological investigation has helped to generate new thinking about the multicultural nature of the Roman Empire in Britain.

Homes and Gardens, the third chapter, considers the domestic origins of many of our conventional ideas about landscape. Early thinking about landscape often equated it with the practice of gardening, and views of countryside were brought into closer perspective when conceptualised as garden-like settings for mansion houses. This is a cultural trait that remains deep in our national psyche, such that the suburban ideal is often defined by the conjunction of homes with neatly ordered gardens.

From the comfort of gardens we move in the fourth chapter to woodlands and forests, landscapes that are equally rooted in the national imagination. Trees and woods are

Above | Tulips growing in the garden at Monk's House, East Sussex, the country home and retreat of Leonard and Virginia Woolf. The garden brought Virginia peace and inspiration, and she had a writing shed in the orchard.

Above | Beach huts at Middle Beach, Studland Bay, Dorset. The 270 huts on this gently shelving, 4-mile stretch of coast are vulnerable to being lost to the sea.

Right | Ashness Farm, a working Lakeland fell farm and sixteenth-century farmhouse in the Lake District, Cumbria.

familiar features of fairy tales and myths, suggesting that they operate as much on the level of the collective subconscious as they do as living, working landscapes. But this is not to underestimate the considerable contribution that wooded landscapes make to people's lives today, as is revealed whenever they are perceived to be under threat.

From the cover of the woods, we move out in the fifth chapter to Open Country. Here we consider the landscape of the everyday farmland and countryside that sits outside of urban areas or country estates. The working country was not always viewed as a suitable subject for the painter's brush, but its picturesque qualities were increasingly recognised in the eighteenth and nineteenth centuries, just as enclosure was curtailing the open character of these landscapes. Movements to protect commons and other open spaces from enclosure gave rise to the formation of the National Trust, which has been particularly associated with the protection of the character of upland landscapes in the Lake District and elsewhere.

Finally, in Shifting Shores we take a landscape perspective to the coast, and look at how it has been imagined and interpreted in the past and present. Given the predominance of maritime themes to many aspects of our history, the coastline often provides a backdrop to patriotic visions of the nation, whether at the White Cliffs of Dover or at Sheringham on the North Norfolk coast. But the uncertainties of rising sea levels and unpredictable geological processes mean that the coast can also be unsettling as a landscape experience. These are places where we are likely to mark the loss of key landscape features, as cliffs erode and harbour walls are beaten back under the waves.

Each chapter includes one or two large-scale works commissioned from award-winning photographer Simon Roberts. Roberts' photographs explore how our collective and national identities are shaped, interpreted, defined and transformed by our relationship with the landscape. Often through expansive, tableau photographs, he creates visual narratives that chart the ambiguities and complexities of post-industrial Britain. The photographs require scrutiny and contemplation. They have a visual command that comes from their expansive nature and scale: all the images are made with a large-format camera. He explains his process:

Where possible I'm looking for a high vantage point from which to frame my photographs, and more often than not this is from the roof of my motorhome (or using a free-standing step ladder when I'm not permitted to park near the scene). As a result, the viewer is often placed at a slight distance and elevation from the subject so they are not part of the action but detached, critical viewers; in essence I attempt to map contemporary life governed by forces that are not possible to see from a position within the crowd. The perspective echoes that of history painting.

Roberts' work explores senses of belonging in landscapes. Since land invariably belongs to somebody, landscape is closely linked to notions of ownership, whether by individuals or by institutions. Land ownership is seldom a simple or exclusive matter, governed in places by a patchwork of title, tenure, covenants, custom and rights of way, as part of landscape's deeply layered history. Landscapes are also linked, beyond legal ownership, to larger worlds of nature and nation, beauty and history, as the term 'belonging' extends to more shared senses of attachment, citizenship and entitlement. The contemporary engagement with landscapes, particularly beauty spots, is also

Ravensglass, Cumbria, 31 July 2014, by Simon Roberts.

linked to older forms of journeying, to pilgrimage. Pleasure seekers follow well-trodden paths to places we call, in a semi-spiritual sense, iconic scenes or national shrines. Just as medieval pilgrimages were sociable as well as spiritual, so visiting landscapes is itself a collective experience: people interact with each other, whether they like it or not, as well as with the places they go to.

The photographs in this book are part of a wider exploration of public interaction with landscapes, and how that frames shared experiences of place and the sense of cultural belonging. Roberts' photographs reveal the degree to which natural-looking landscapes are peopled by various groups – hikers here, picnickers there – and the degree to which the landscape is managed and shaped for visiting as well as for other commercial activities such as farming and forestry. The photographs explore how people perform in such places, whether striking out into the landscape, taking in the view, or observing other visitors. This is the nation as a people as well as a place, its landscape a social theatre as well as picturesque scenery. Says Roberts:

In most of these photographs we see the somewhat mundane ways in which we interact with the landscape – diving into a river, cycling along a towpath – interacting with the landscape perhaps with no sense of the historic significance of the place we're passing through or using. I'm also looking for subliminal signals in the landscape and often there is a sense of tension just under the surface of my photograph – the police car in Kielder Water, the jockeying for position to take a picture at Flatford Mill, the managed pathways at Stonehenge, the gas delivery van 'spoiling' the view of Sheringham Park.

Let us look more closely at the photograph opposite. Here is a canonical Lake District view, along Wastwater (the deepest lake in England) and towards Scafell Pike (the highest mountain). The photograph includes in the foreground a group of visitors, teenage girls. The girls have turned away from the sublime scene in view to huddle around the screen of a mobile phone. Similarly, our attention is focused as much on them as the view. What, we might ask, are they up to? Are they looking at a photograph they have taken of the scene behind them? Are they, like more geographically minded visitors, consulting a digital map of the area? Or are they texting a friend, perhaps sending a view of the scene or, more likely, a selfie? Or are they chatting to a person in another place, wishing themselves away from the landscape they have been brought to in the family car? Since the Lake District was first regarded over two centuries ago as 'a sort of national property', to use Wordsworth's phrase, its fells have silently witnessed many such figures. This is a portrait as well as a landscape, a social as well as natural scene, a people in their place, as well as a view of the landscape itself.

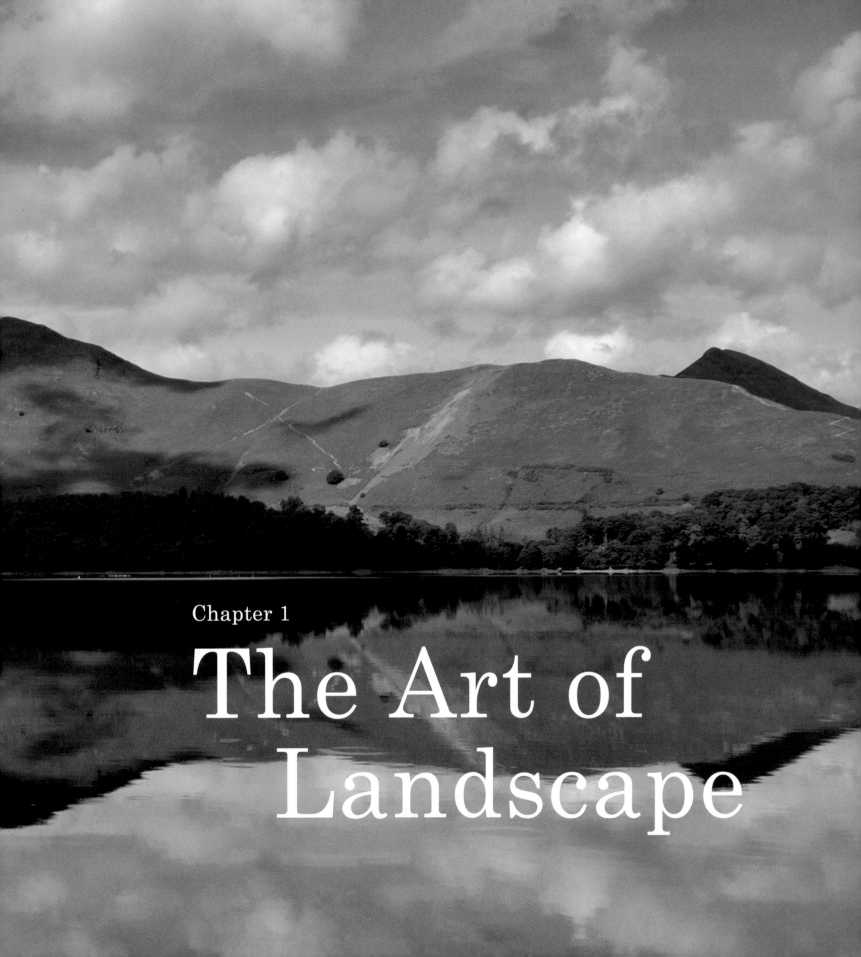

Chapter 1

The Art of Landscape

Our views of the landscape are powerfully shaped by art, whether we are aware of it or not. In Britain there is an especially strong tradition of representing landscape through painting, as well as through poetry, novels, film, photography and music. Landscape art is endlessly popular, whether hanging from the walls of national collections or available in mass reproductions on postcards and in the background of television costume dramas. A similar artistry is displayed in plans and designs for shaping and managing land. The tradition of using land itself as a medium was especially vibrant in the eighteenth century, in the form of landscape gardening, and remains with us today in the practices of contemporary artists and landscape architects.

The landscape arts shape our decisions about which places we feel are worth visiting and valuing. The depiction of sites in art breeds a certain cultural familiarity with those scenes, encouraging us to visit them and experience them directly. Some landscapes, like the Lake District or the River Thames, have been so repeatedly represented over the centuries that their many layers of literary or pictorial associations can be uncovered just as we might excavate on the ground their material archaeology and geology. Yet the art of landscape can also be double-edged: even while celebrating the beauty and enchantment of rural and urban scenes, they reveal a darker side, showing us poverty or oppressive social relations.

This chapter takes the form of a journey to places that eloquently express the art of landscape and its relationship to other modes of landscape appreciation, from gardening and hill walking to mapping and tourism. It shows that landscapes can be experienced both as deeply familiar, lived-in places, and as less familiar sites to visit – landscape as both roots and routes. And it demonstrates how art and culture are central to our understanding of what landscape is and might be. We begin in the hilly regions of Britain, which have long been valued for their landscape beauty.

Above | James Walker Tucker, *Hiking, c.*1936, tempera on panel, Laing Art Gallery. The hikers are in the Cotswolds reading a new Popular Edition Ordnance Survey map.

Sublime Scenery

The 'sublime' has long been understood to mean a quality of greatness or grandeur that inspires awe and wonder. From the seventeenth century onwards the concept and the emotions it evokes have been a source of inspiration for artists and writers, particularly in relation to the natural landscape, in its wilder, more dramatic forms: soaring peaks, rushing torrents, rain-swept moors, stormy seas – echoed in the title of the most sublime-sounding record in rock, 'River Deep, Mountain High'.

Since the taste for mountain scenery developed in the eighteenth century, upland regions in Britain have proved a lure for artists, keen to test and extend their skills and techniques. A fashion for open-air painting and sketching followed closely in the wake of others, such as the early map makers who were keen to survey once forbidding-looking and unruly regions. As its name suggests, the Ordnance Survey began as a military operation, to survey the Highlands of Scotland for troop movements and fortification, in the wake of the Jacobite rebellions. The maps produced were themselves highly esteemed as works of graphic art.

Artists both then and since have engaged with maps and their imaginative potential, if only to make new kinds of cartography that go beyond visual conventions or to tell different stories of land and life. Maps themselves have been adapted and marketed for a wide range of pursuits. This includes art that expresses the civil and peaceable pursuits of hiking from the inter-war period of the last century, when people from all social backgrounds raised their eyes to the hills with a view to ascending them and the fells were alive to the sight and sound of climbers and ramblers.

The region of England's highest hills, the Lake District, is a well-loved landscape. So admired are these uplands, and by so many different interests, that they are a case study of how different approaches to landscape – whether appreciation, conservation or management – might be accommodated. Literature of all kinds, from the romantic visions of Coleridge and Wordsworth to the children's books of Arthur Ransome and Beatrix Potter, has played a decisive role in shaping the reputation of the Lakes, and framing other pursuits, from farming to climbing.

The Lake District was first 'discovered' in the late eighteenth century by tourists, artists and the owners of fashionable villas (the holiday homes of their day), all eager to see this pleasing landscape. Most visitors then, as now, stayed close to the main roads, gathering at fashionable scenic spots marked on popular maps and in guidebooks. Here, views across the landscape were governed by reference to landscape paintings – the more 'picturesque', the better.

Above | Map reading at Great Langdale, Cumbria.

More adventurous spirits ventured by foot further into the fells, in search of emotionally uplifting visions and feelings in the 'sublime' forms of landscape, of soaring peaks and plunging vales. J. M. W. Turner was among the most well travelled of painters within and beyond Britain, depicting all manner of landscapes at a time of profound social and environmental transformation. Drawing on his sketching tour of the Lakes, the young artist staged a dramatic spectacle at the Royal Academy in 1798 with a pair of highly atmospheric sublime scenes: one of Buttermere after a storm, arced by a rainbow, and one of the mists rising from Coniston Fells at sunrise. These were much more than mere documentary scenes – indeed, many of the features were sampled from a range of sources, designed to provoke suitably awe-inspiring scenographic effects.

In its unusual vertical format *Morning Amongst the Coniston Fells* (1798) projects the vertiginous qualities of bright towering peaks and darkened dales. The suspended viewpoint, in the tradition of such elevated views, is an imaginative one, with spectators looking down to Coniston Water from a crag, higher than the shepherd below with his flock dares go. The painting was further elevated as an artwork by a quotation included in the catalogue from Milton's epic poem Paradise Lost:

Left | Visitors to the Lakes contemplate the scenery from Friar's Crag, a promontory jutting into Derwentwater, which was given to the National Trust in 1920.

Left | J. W. M. Turner, *Morning Amongst the Coniston Fells, Cumberland*, exhibited 1798, oil on canvas, Tate.

...Ye mists and exhalations that now rise
From hill or streaming lake, dusky or gray,
Till the sun paints your fleecy skirts with gold,
In honour to the world's great Author, rise.

The implication is that the scene is a primeval wilderness, paradise found.

Turner scrambled higher than most painters, but it was the Lakeland poets who popularised fell walking as an extreme pursuit, leading to the very summits. With flask and knapsack, Samuel Taylor Coleridge pioneered recreational rock scrambling and peak experiences in his excursion in the summer of 1802, scribbling notes and sketch maps as he went. He achieved the first recorded climb of Scafell Pike, the most 'sublime & commanding elevation in England'. To do so, he ventured beyond the pasture line, and tracks of shepherds, up the bare rock. Deciding to make a direct route towards Eskdale, he then made a hair-raising descent, down precipitous gulleys and waterfalls from which there was no return – and past the ominous remains of a lost sheep. Safely at an inn, he sent a long impressive message of his heroic derring-do to the object of his romantic love, Sara Hutchinson, revelling in his bodily experience: he was, he wrote, 'calm and fearless and confident' while 'my Limbs were all in a tremble', and stripping off to the waist he found a sweat rash covering 'the whole of my Breast from my Neck to my Navel'.

Above | Unlike Coleridge, today's walkers can follow Scafell Pike Trail, built by National Trust teams from Wasdale Head to Hollow Stones.

Left | Lingmell Gill tumbles over a rocky bed down the west side of Scafell Pike.

Right | View over Wastwater at Wasdale, Cumbria. Due to the popularity of walking in the Lake District, stiles and managed paths have become a normal part of the landscape.

Like many apparently solitary forms of landscape appreciation, the sublime is more sociable than it seems. In the wake of Coleridge, guidebooks surveyed safer ways on Scafell for walkers, while the poet's descent is still a route that figures in the modern rock climber's catalogue. Climbing was regarded from the beginning as an elevated cultural pursuit in more ways than one: an art form as well as a sport, a skilled character-building activity, and a close encounter with nature by contrast to the passive spectatorship of trippers below. Like the gentlemanly sports of cricket and horse racing, climbing generated commemorative art and literature. Photographers were on hand to record both the climbs and the alpine-dressed climbers as they moved out on to more exposed routes, on to the open ridges, slabs and walls. They also produced shock-inducing postcards of dramatic ascents for the souvenir shops. Fell and rock climbing claimed the peaks for wider cultural heritage, the summits of Scafell Pike and Great Gable being presented to the National Trust as memorials to men killed in the First World War.

The culture of climbing broadened its social participation after the Second World War, as the outdoors movement to the hills from northern industrial towns expanded from hiking and scrambling to rock climbing, and the ascent of peaks renewed its radically Romantic, bohemian edge. Climbing was likened to an act of avant-garde imagination, with routes compared to artworks, created, authored, named and dated, assessed and graded. Classic climbs are now highly valued, and like overused footpaths have a measure of physical protection.

Climbing has inspired artistic responses too. The artist-climber Dan Shipsides draws on the idea of 'the line' that a new route-maker perceives on a rock, stitching a way with rope as he progresses, his body movements creating the shape. Shipsides' gallery installations include photographic-based drawings of classic, breakthrough pioneering climbs, such as *Zig Zag (Puttrell c.1900)* on Kinder Scout, which highlights the shape of the route created by the climb itself.

Romantic feelings for mountain scenery can be found dwelling in the vales and dales as well as scaling the fells and peaks, a sensibility pioneered in the writings of Wordsworth. Born and raised in the Lake District, the 29-year-old-poet returned from Germany in 1799 to make his home in Grasmere, in the house now called Dove Cottage. Here for the next decade Wordsworth produced many of his finest works, which have helped to define the region as a literary landscape.

Above | Abraham Brothers, 'Climbers on Napes Needle', original print Fell & Rock Climbing Club and Abbot Hall. This prominent rock spire on Great Gable was first climbed by Walter Parry Haskett Smith in 1886. His ascent ushered in the modern concept of rock climbing, whereby climbers could look at crags and pinnacles as sporting challenges in their own right, rather than as preparation for tackling Alpine summits.

Left | Great Gable with its summit wreathed in cloud. In 1923 the Fell & Rock Climbing Club purchased 12 fells in the central lakes, including Great Gable, and donated them to the National Trust. A cast bronze memorial on the summit commemorates the members of the club who were killed in the First World War.

Left | Wordsworth's study as visitors find it today at Allan Bank, Grasmere, Cumbria. Literary friends Thomas de Quincey and Samuel Taylor Coleridge were frequent visitors during the few years the Wordsworth family lived here.

Visiting painters hitherto presented the embowering vale of Grasmere as a pastoral paradise. In their writings and actions, Wordsworth and his sister Dorothy reclaimed Grasmere, replacing superficial sightseeing with serious careful observation, even a sense of religious and moral observance. Here the Wordsworths cultivated an outlook that was attentive to the commonplace, in both the natural and the social world. They retold stories of the seasons and of the poor who made their living in the landscape, and offered a vision that extended from their cottage garden to the vale as a whole, enclosed by sheltering hills.

Wordsworth's writings have come to shape Lakeland as a source of artistic inspiration, even for those whose knowledge of his verse does not extend much beyond lines on clouds and daffodils. This Romantic vision tends to foreclose much of the middle ground of the pictorial landscape view. Instead the imagination is released to focus on what the poet called the presence of nature, whether in the humble detail of the near at hand or the grandeur of the far away, extending in scope from the aerial domain of clouds and birds to the earthly ground of plants and flowers. This is an encircling sense of place and space, the epic intersecting with the everyday.

Above | An artist creates her own interpretation of the view over Grasmere from one of the windows at Allan Bank.

A rich archive of manuscript verse, letters and diaries is now deposited at Dove Cottage, which has become a place of study and creativity for those wishing to research and reimagine this Romantic landscape vision. The scope and complexity of Wordsworth's domestic vision has, in this way, been opened up. The wider, social context of the time was one of global conflict and national emergency during the Napoleonic Wars – a world of loss and grief, displacement and anxiety. Wordsworth's poems from this period do not confine themselves to local matters, but range widely to address questions of political liberty in places as far apart as Venice, Switzerland and the Caribbean.

Wordsworth moved house for his growing family in 1810, to a merchant's villa in Grasmere, Allan Bank – which, ironically, he had once condemned as an eyesore. In the same year, he published the first edition of his own *Guide to Lakes*. This educational text combined quotations from his own verse with detailed observations on natural and social history, climate and community, and became a conservationist rallying call for the region to be regarded as a 'national property', one to be defended from development. Appointed Poet Laureate in 1845, Wordsworth enjoyed a late career as the national bard and Grand Old Man of the Lakes. Not surprisingly, the region soon became known as Wordsworth Country, and after his death the poet was revered, considered almost a saint and worshipper of nature. People made pilgrimages to his various houses and the places mentioned in his verse. Dove Cottage was purchased as a memorial, a literary shrine – the third such writer's house to be bought for the nation after Shakespeare's birthplace in Stratford upon Avon and Milton's house in Chalfont St Giles. This was part of a movement to revere the 'homes and haunts' of English authors, where the presence of their former artistic occupants could still be felt. It was part of a wider idea, the spirit of place, defining whole regions of England as signature landscapes, from Wordsworth Country to Constable Country.

Below | The house at Allan Bank, where Wordsworth lived from 1810. Opened to the public since 2012, visitors are encouraged to explore their own creativity in words and images.

Natural Wonders

Landscape is sometimes on such a scale that it can't fail to provoke feelings of wonder, awe and reverence. Mountainous country had once been considered wild and unruly, but by the eighteenth century it was increasingly sought out for the emotions that it stirred. That sense of the sublime and the majestic, which made the uplands of England and Wales so popular with domestic tourists, can be found in other places too: the folds of sweeping hillsides, epic cliffs and coastal promontories, and distinctive rock formations. The National Trust looks after many examples of such natural wonders, valued greatly for their beauty and splendour.

Above | Pen y Fan, Brecon Beacons, Powys. A view from the Brecon Beacons, featuring the road to Pen y Fan, South Wales's highest mountain. The peak was gifted to the Trust in 1965 by Sir Brian Mountain, Chairman of the Eagle Star Insurance Company. There is public access across the whole area, and its popularity creates conservation challenges (such as maintaining footpaths).

Left | Wasdale, Scafell, Cumbria. Walkers on the Scafell path with Wastwater in the distance. Scafell Pike is the highest mountain in England, and was given to the nation as a memorial to Lakelanders who died in the First World War. Coleridge called it the most 'sublime & commanding elevation in England'.

Above | A view of the coastline looking east from the summit of Golden Cap in Dorset. In the foreground the heather is in bloom. The Jurassic Coast stretches for nearly a hundred miles from west Devon to east Dorset, and was the UK's second designated wholly natural World Heritage Site after the Giant's Causeway.

Left | Henrhyd Falls, Brecon Beacons, Powys. Its white veil of water cascades over the stratified rock face and into the valley below where it continues to flow in amongst boulders downstream. Waterfalls became objects of great interest to tourists of the 'picturesque' in the later eighteenth century.

Right | Brimham Rocks, Nidderdale, North Yorkshire. The millstone grit sandstone has been sculpted by glaciation, wind and rain into this collection of weird and wonderful rock formations, earning them nicknames such as Dancing Bear, The Eagle and The Gorilla. Standing at a height of 30 metres, they offer outstanding views over the surrounding area.

Left | Giant's Causeway, County Antrim,. The polygonal basalt columns at Giant's Causeway were created by an ancient volcanic eruption. Interest in the causeway was greatly promoted by Frederick Hervey, 4th Earl of Bristol, who was also Bishop of Derry. The Earl Bishop, as he was known, cut the path that now leads down to the rocks.

Right | White Cliffs of Dover, Kent. The Cliffs mark the point where the North Downs meet the sea, resulting in the spectacular chalk cliff-face. They were immortalised in Vera Lynn's recording of the song '(There'll be Bluebirds Over) The White Cliffs of Dover', and continue to evoke patriotic associations today.

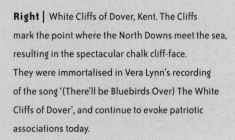

Above | John Constable, *Flatford Mill* (*'Scene on a Navigable River'*), 1816–17, oil on canvas, Tate.

Lowlands

If the lowlands of eastern England have attracted fewer artists, writers and tourists than the uplands of the west and north, those they have inspired have proved highly discerning ones. This flat, fertile country, with its slow rivers and muddy estuaries, has been highly valued for its fertile farming, yet lacks some of the literary and artistic heritage of other parts. The work of John Constable, and the making of Constable Country on the Suffolk–Essex border, is the great exception.

Constable's painting of Suffolk was as radical in its way as Wordsworth's poetry of Cumbria. Rather than reinterpreting a well-known place, however, it brought to light a landscape that was hitherto unknown to art and which was well off the tourist track. The valley of the River Stour was mainly valued by practically minded men for

Below | Willy Lott's House on the River Stour, Suffolk. The house appears in several of Constable's paintings, including *The Mill Stream*, *The White Horse* and *The Hay Wain*.

its agriculture and navigation – not least Constable's father, a miller and merchant based at Flatford. Constable brought to his art a range and depth of detailed personal experience and a practical understanding of the workaday world, from farming to canal navigation, at a place where the river became tidal and where his father exported corn and imported coal. Constable depicted places little known to a London art market, but with sufficient allusions to the paintings of the old masters to make them appealing, particularly the canalised waterways, big skies and wide horizons of Dutch art. He made large pictures of small places, to make the mundane more monumental.

Visitors to Constable Country, as it came to be called in his own lifetime, are often surprised at how small it first seems on the ground. Many of the sites of his major pictures are located within a few yards of Flatford Mill. The scale tends to shift, as it does in lowland scenery, when adopting a vantage point a few feet above ground level –

on a bridge, or on a mill forecourt – as the painter often did. In the past 20 years, many of the views have been cleared of blocking trees and vegetation so that the landscape on the ground now reflects Constable's pictures. The paintings, however, were in turn the product of the artist's own imaginary editing of the landscape, assembled from a variety of sources rather than being direct representations of reality. Many were recollections of childhood scenes, bigger in memory than they probably seemed to the artist when he visited from London, where he lived and exhibited for most of his life.

The sense of movement felt in Constable's pictures is experienced at walking pace, following footpaths, cart tracks and towpaths. Visitors to Flatford Mill today are invited to do the same when they leave the car park, wandering down the artist's memory lanes and activating some collective memories and myths of the present. Day trippers to Constable Country may know little more of the painter's art than that reproduced on tea trays and calendars, images of rural retreat and timeless scenes that somehow stand apart from the busy modern world. Such scenes have a power beyond the merely decorative, however. As landscapes, Constable's art speaks to people from all backgrounds, and from countries well beyond England. To some, Constable's fields and meadows seem strangely familiar, an echo or far cry from places where land is still

Above | The dry dock beside the River Stour at Flatford. Stour lighters (barges) would have rested on the wooden stocks while being constructed or repaired. The dock was restored in 1988 using Constable's drawings and paintings. It is one of three docks that are known to have operated at Flatford when Constable was a boy.

Left | Visitors to the National Trust site compare Constable's paintings with the scene at Flatford Mill.

Willy Lott's House at Flatford, East Bergholt, Suffolk, 20 July 2014 by Simon Roberts.

traditionally farmed. Constable Country, whether hung on the walls of homes or experienced 'for real' at Flatford, offers a sense of dwelling and belonging. The restoration and refurbishment of Flatford Mill – first as an artist's studio and then as an educational field-study centre for scientific as well as artistic learning – helps to draw attention to the investigative nature of Constable's art. As was the case with Wordsworth, a focus on domesticity and ideas of rural retreat risk obscuring the wider connections that Constable's art reveals.

Further to the north of lowland England, at the furthest reach of Lincolnshire, lies a richly cultivated valley landscape, one that is largely overlooked by tourists and artists, since it is not conventionally beautiful or pictorial, and is well off the beaten track. The River Ancholme runs across a level plain to the Humber Estuary, and for its last 20 miles its once meandering course is straightened into a canalised watercourse heading due north, direct as a compass needle. This is landscape reclaimed for commercial life from a shifting, marshy waterland, one subject to successive large-scale schemes of enclosure, a place with physical and cultural connections to the continental lowlands across the North Sea. Here are the so-called carrlands. Their name derives from the Danish *kjaar* and refers to the marshes and bogs and seasonal pastures that once offered a habitation and livelihood for people and wildlife, but which now serve as drained riverside fields of commercial agriculture. Here is a highly planned and engineered landscape of locks, quays, weirs, cuts, sluices and iron bridges, which in places stretches forlorn and half-abandoned. Elsewhere, nature reserves have been newly converted from the melancholic landscapes of formerly industrialised farms and fields.

Above | Mike Pearson's work explores the planned and engineered landscape of the carrlands of Lincolnshire, with their straightened watercourses and drainage management.

These carrlands are being reclaimed by others too, including artists. Performance artist Mike Pearson's sound work *Carrlands* reclaims this abandoned landscape, revealing its hidden histories. The narrator of the work tells various episodes of carrland history, weaving in words of the past from historical documents and his own personal memories. The various movements offer excursions into a landscape that is physically difficult for a visitor to traverse. The episodes of Carrlands are not told in a smoothly continuous chronological way, but present sometimes surprising juxtapositions of fact and fiction, history and memory. The bridge at Horkstow Carrs, for example, was one of the earliest suspension bridges in Britain, designed in the 1820s as part of a wider project of reclamation. It now stands somewhat forlornly off road by the ruins of abandoned brickworks, overtaken by subsequent waves of development.

As well as modern bricks and ancient bog oaks, we hear here of a more familiar tradition in the English art of landscape. We picture eighteenth-century painter George Stubbs' residency at Horkstow to study the anatomy of a horse carcass – a key part of the artist's modern, scientific-minded view of country life. And we hear the work of early 20th-century composer and song-collector Percy Grainger, who was key to successive

English folk revivals. This includes the murder ballad he collected here, 'Horkstow Grange', in which waggoner John Bowlin kills the miser Steeleye Span. Works of art like this help to draw out the many different points of connection residing within a landscape, even one as seemingly dull and featureless as that of the Lincolnshire carrs.

Before the dykes were made, and the river bed changed, when the carrs were nobbut bog-lands, an' full o' watter-holes, when this was a land of great meres of black water, and creeping trickles of green water, of squishy mools as'd suck owt in, a wild desolate dreary marsh, full of strange sights and sounds, a land teeming with bogles and boggarts and Will-o'-the Wykes and Jack a' Lanterns and such like, uncanny dwellers, crawling horrors, slithery things, shapeless worms, the green coated strangers, hands without arms, rotting flesh dropping from their mouldy bones, and the voices of dead people that came in the darklins, moaning and crying and beckoning, all night thruff, tod-lowries dancing on the tussocks, wall-eyed woe-women, and witches riding on the great black snags, the trunks of bog oaks, twisted and bent, that still protruded in the undrained landscape, that turned to snakes, and raced with them in the water as they wailed round isolated houses and rattled the latches...

Above | Horkstow Bridge, a fine example of one of the earliest suspension bridges, now stands neglected and all but forgotten.

Left | A dyke at Horkstow is slowly being reclaimed by nature, in contrast to the managed waterways in the photograph opposite.

The Creative Spirit

A sense of landscape emerges from the relationship between people and places. It is both an inspiration for the creative process and a product of that process. Who can visit Flatford Mill in Suffolk without being reminded of John Constable's art? Or walk the Lake District without Wordsworth's poetry coming to mind? It is no surprise, therefore, to reflect on the fact that many of the National Trust's special landscapes and places have connections to individual artists, writers or composers. Just as their artistic visions were drawn from the landscape, so an appreciation of their work helps us to understand and respond to their places today.

Above | Virginia's Woolf's writing shed in the orchard at Monk's House, East Sussex. Virginia and Lionel Woolf made their home here in 1919. Virginia wrote that it 'will be our address for ever and ever; indeed, I've already marked out our graves in the yard which joins our meadow'.

Left | Thomas Hardy's house, Max Gate in Dorchester, Dorset, where the novelist wrote some of his most famous books including *Tess of the d'Urbervilles* and *Jude the Obscure*. Hardy designed the house in 1885, and discovered an ancient burial in the foundations. A hundred years later it was revealed that a late Neolithic causeway enclosure lay beneath the grounds: appropriate enough, for a writer so entranced by the sacred Wessex landscape.

Above | Lamb House in Rye, East Sussex, is a house with many literary associations. Henry James lived and wrote here. After his death in 1916, it became home to E.F. Benson and his brother A.C. Benson, both also writers. E.F. Benson was inspired to write his Mapp and Lucia series at Lamb House, in a room that was destroyed by a bomb in 1940.

Left | The White Garden at Sissinghurst in Kent. The house and gardens were restored by Vita Sackville-West and her husband Harold Nicolson in the 1930s. Their grandson, Adam Nicolson, has written of the castle, his childhood home, that it is 'the most precious thing I know', and that it is the place where he came to understand 'what a landscape was'.

Below | The oriel window with the doorway beneath on the south elevation of Lacock Abbey, Wiltshire. The three oriel windows on the south elevation were built by William Henry Fox Talbot during the years 1827–30. It was in the South Gallery that Fox Talbot took what is perhaps the earliest surviving photographic negative.

Above | Hill Top, in Sawrey, near Ambleside, Cumbria, has a special place in the history of the National Trust. Beatrix Potter bought this seventeenth-century farmhouse in 1905 with the proceeds of *The Tale of Peter Rabbit*. She subsequently left it to the Trust along with a substantial area of farmland, having used the proceeds of her children's books to purchase other properties for the Trust in the Lake District.

Left | Leith Hill has long been a popular draw for visitors seeking to take in the views across the Surrey Hills. Leith Hill Place has associations with a number of famous figures. It was once owned by the Wedgwood family, and was regularly visited by Charles Darwin who conducted experiments in the grounds. Later it was the childhood home of English composer Ralph Vaughan Williams.

Above | George Bernard Shaw's Edwardian villa – Shaw's Corner – is hidden deep in the Hertfordshire countryside, at Ayot St Lawrence. Shaw lived here for forty years, before bequeathing the house and its grounds to the National Trust. This writing hut is still on display in the garden; it revolves so as to improve the light or vary the view.

Maritime Scenes

The art of landscape in Britain has never been far from the sea. Coastal scenes were a popular subject for landscape painters, but artists also dwelled imaginatively on the more global, oceanic art of overseas exploration, including trade and naval battles and the portrayal of overseas lands from the Caribbean to India. Landscape art in this way spoke of Britain's role as a self-consciously maritime nation. The power of the ocean itself, its depths, distances and dangers, raises the sublime register of such scenes. The art of landscape was carried overseas, along with other cultural accomplishments, to depict – and so domesticate – very different places, describing strange lands in a familiar language. The traffic in representation has proved two-way, with cosmopolitan culture, particularly in port cities, providing new material for the landscape arts in a range of media, including film and music. Maritime scenes have a renewed profile at present, as a matter of cultural heritage at a time when Britain is no longer a global oceanic power.

Mythically and materially, oceanic islands have played a key role in our imagination, holding up a mirror to the island nation at home. They have been projected either as utopias where social restraints might be loosened or (and often at the same time) as licentious places badly in need of law and order and the blessings of European development and civilization. The origins of the English novel, after all, lie on Robinson's Crusoe's island. Daniel Defoe's narrative describes the castaway's experiences on the island where he was shipwrecked, his landing, exploration, encounter and settlement, and it imports the Protestant work ethic that Defoe also describes in his travel books on Britain. Defoe's other adventure stories – of shadier seaborne characters, of pirates and privateers such as Captain Singleton and his voyage to Madagascar – engage with a wider literature in fact and fiction. Stephanie Jones from Southampton University has explored the fluid legal status of lands in this period when rivalry was not only between imperial powers, but between the claims of state and private commercial interests, not to mention the powers of the peoples who already occupied those treasure islands.

Visual artists, along with map makers, accompanied major voyages of exploration. As scholars piloted by Geoff Quilley from the National Maritime Museum have shown, they helped to survey the coasts, to document new flora and fauna, and to

Above | The south front of Anglesey Abbey in Cambridgeshire. Between 1926 and 1966. The 1st Lord Fairhaven transformed this former Augustinian Priory into a country home and built up a collection of high-quality eighteenth- and nineteenth-century artworks and sculptures.

represent newly found countries and climates, lands and peoples, discovering exotic nature and culture and describing its transformation by European trade, settlement and colonization. Styles of picture-making which had been developed for the form and atmosphere of European landscapes were now redeveloped to accommodate, with varying degrees of conviction, these unfamiliar human and physical geographies.

The most glamorous of voyages were those of Captain Cook to the South Seas, in the late eighteenth century, marked by an enlightened spirit of scientific endeavour and tragic misunderstandings. One place in particular became a byword for exotic

Below | The Ship Bedroom at Anglesey Abbey, where William Hodges' painting *View of Oaitepeha Bay, Tahiti*, 1776, hangs.

otherness, of paradise found, and lost: Tahiti. A key image of Cook's voyage to Tahiti hangs well inland in one of the National Trust's country houses: Anglesey Abbey, Cambridgeshire. It is part of an art collection of maritime scenes, which were assembled in the twentieth century and are now displayed in the Ship Bedroom. *View of Oaitepeha Bay, Tahiti* is by the leading artist on board Cook's ship *Resolution*, William Hodges. Based on sketches made during a two-week visit in 1773, it was worked up into an oil painting back in London two years later for exhibition at the Royal Academy. In the process, documentary observations of the Tahitian landscape and people have been remixed with classical European artistic conventions and associations.

The rocky mountain landscape and tree-fringed bay are real enough, if shown in a Mediterranean light. The bathing figures in the foreground recall the naked nymphs of classical mythology, while the tattooed buttocks of the half-draped seated woman signal both an ethnographic fascination with native body decoration and, no less fascinating to a London audience, the erotic reputation of Tahitians for English sailors. Richly luxuriant, a libidinal landscape, it seems a tropical paradise. At the same time, there is something unsettling in the scene, signs of trouble in paradise. In the middle distance is a scene of death, an elevated platform bearing a shrouded corpse. Such intimations of mortality, of the transience of earthly pleasures are familiar in European art, but here signal a more disquieting cultural encounter. For flanking the foreground figure, and framing the entire scene, is a forbidding-looking idol, looking less an ethnographic artefact destined for a European museum, and more an animating, ancestral spirit of the place. Tahitians were recognised by Europeans as culturally advanced peoples, skilled in trade and war, and not entirely subject to imperial reimaginings. Complex, disturbing images such as this reminded Europeans of the limits as well as the opportunities of scientific, commercial and sexual curiosity.

On the Waterfront

Most large cities in Britain have been built by water, on major tidal rivers, facing outwards to the sea and a global world of trade, and inwards along a network of waterways to a hinterland of farming and industry. Waterways are perhaps no longer the major route ways for cities as workaday worlds, as social and economic places, but waterfronts often offer the best vantage points for appreciating their historic character, their major sites and scenery. This is why waterfront regeneration is such a central part of urban heritage planning, revealing cities as landscapes, with striking scenic views and sites such as castles, docks and palaces which have long complex histories and extensive geographical connections. And far along such major waterways, we may not actually be able to see the city but we can often sense it, its cultural reach and significance – upstream in rural places where the mansions of successful merchants and financiers stand on the bankside, and downriver, beyond estuary mudflats where shipping plies its course.

Despite, or perhaps because of its decline as a major transatlantic port, Liverpool today celebrates a cosmopolitan, maritime heritage and maintains a strong sense of pride. It celebrates being a place often seen as peripheral, even exceptional, to mainland England, creative in a community-conscious and slightly contrary way. Its heritage includes not just its built environment (the docks were restored as a cultural landscape with galleries and museums), but also its music, the sounds of a city that became famous in the mid-1960s for a distinctive style of music named after the tidal river of its waterfront: Merseybeat.

The myths and realities of Liverpool's seafaring culture have shaped understandings of Merseybeat, including the migration of Irish music, the folk revival of sea shanties, and the import of rare American country, blues and rock 'n' roll records by its merchant mariners, the so-called Cunard Cowboys. In musical terms, as a conduit of outside influences, the Mersey has been imagined as a tributary of the Mississippi and that other major port city Hamburg. In the sixties, Merseybeat was a multi-media movement, shaped by the music industry, including the press, management and public relations. It was more than a sound; in the phrase of the time, it was a 'scene', a cultural landscape of venues, fashion and attitude. And it drew on a wider national fascination with 'northern' cities and characters, then being depicted in films, plays and novels.

Left | The Museum of Liverpool stands on the city's famous waterfront, its purpose is to tell the story of Liverpool and its people, and the city's wider global significance.

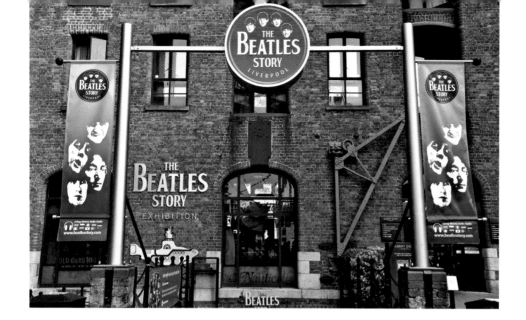

As Peter Coates observes in his book *A Story of Six Rivers*, Liverpool and the Mersey took on the earlier cultural reputation of Vienna and the Danube as popular musical landscapes. 'Early twentieth century pilgrimages to the sites where "The Blue Danube" Waltz was written and first performed have been superseded by treks to Liverpool's Cavern Club where the Beatles performed, the boyhood homes of Lennon and McCartney, and the locations that feature in songs such as "Penny Lane".'

The artistry of the Beatles' music, including their literate lyrics and image, arguably owed more to art school than to seaman's taverns, more to the suburbs in which Lennon and McCartney were brought up than to dockland terraces. If performing in the sleazy clubs of Hamburg for drunken sailors honed their stagecraft, the group's image, including their distinctive hairstyle, was shaped by that city's middle-class bohemian fringe. Their songs about Liverpool were composed long after they left it and became, along with the fashion for Edwardian antiques and imagined childhood, part of the nostalgic strain of Swinging London.

An exhibition entitled 'The Beat Goes On' was held in 2008 as part of Liverpool's programme as a European City of Culture. It revealed a wider, more deep-rooted musical world of Merseyside, excavating cultural memories before the 1960s and bringing the story forward to include recent, more locally important but less nationally known music. In partnership with Liverpool University's Institute of Popular Music, the exhibition revealed music-scapes that lay well beyond the sites and sounds of Merseybeat, a more underground, 'intangible heritage' characterising the urban environment. Displays charted the often shifting world of music-making, performance and recording, often in temporary venues and often leaving little trace.

Further south, the landscape of London is decisively shaped by the River Thames. This national river flows from the rural heartland of Gloucestershire and Oxfordshire to the North Sea, staging a magnificent show of civic power as it passes through the city, past its palaces and power stations, under its many splendid bridges. It is often overlooked

that Wordsworth and Constable, the champions of upland and lowland countryside respectively, both converged on the Thames to celebrate the city's prosperity and prospects, and its connection to a wider world of nature and nation.

So Wordsworth declared in *Upon Westminster Bridge* (1802):

Earth has not anything to show more fair:
Dull would he be of soul who could pass by
A sight so touching in its majesty:
The City now doth, like a garment, wear
The beauty of the morning; silent, bare,
Ships, towers, domes, theatres, and temples lie
Open unto the fields, and to the sky;
All bright and glittering in the smokeless air.

It is a poem that renovated a repertoire of established views of London, including Tudor images of Thameside pageantry and Canaletto's sparkling paintings of the city made a century before.

Left | Abandoned cruise missile shelters, Greenham Common, from Patrick Keiller's film *Robinson in Ruins*, 2010.

Thirty years later, when Constable painted his great panorama of London, *The Opening of Waterloo Bridge*, there was little of Wordsworth's 'smokeless air' to be seen, with the South Bank so industrialised. The painter makes a point of showing the black smoke from the chimneys as part of the patriotic spectacle of a bridge renamed to celebrate a famous war victory. It is an equivocal picture: the smoke contrasting with the billowing clouds over London is a knowledgeable observation of urban meteorology, at a time when weather watchers were conscious of the effects of smoke pollution in a changing climate. Indeed its vantage point is the Bankside house of a leading anti-smoke campaigner. This is a picture of mixed messages, telling many stories. Painted in 1832, at a time of tumultuous political reform, it looks back loyally to a commemorative event staged 15 years before, with the royal flotilla gathering at Whitehall Stairs.

Artists of all kinds have continued to probe the power of the landscape of London along the Thames. The very pollution of the riverside atmosphere – the smoggy banks and dockside lanes, and their mysterious effects – attracted painters, writers and poets. Monet's impressionism was shaped as much by his murky scenes on the Thames as by his more sparkling ones along the Seine, as much by his homage to Turner's many views of the London river as by what he actually saw. Visions of London have been shaped by watery worlds, haunted by the prospect of rising damp from its groundwater and underground rivers, as well as by mist and rain, and by flood risk, especially now in a time of rising sea levels. London has proved to be, in the phrase of writer Iain Sinclair, a 'liquid city'.

Filmmaker Patrick Keiller has explored the sometimes hidden currents of power of London, of its political state as well as its commercial networks. His fictional Robinson travels to places throughout the Thames Valley. *London* (1994) explores the capital, across its major sites and scenes, and goes in search of literary and artistic byways, making a notable excursion across main roads, housing estates and recreation grounds down the River Brent, a tributary of the Thames on the unfashionable if cosmopolitan outskirts of the capital from Brent Cross to Brentford. The itinerary of *Robinson in*

Ruins (2010) is circumscribed, centring on Oxfordshire, but attentive to long-standing, wide-ranging, networks of metropolitan power. By contrast, *Robinson in Space* (1997) begins with a trip downriver from Reading to the Thames Estuary at Sheerness, before striking out on six journeys to other major ports and their hinterlands of manufacture, distribution and storage.

Robinson in Space takes in riverside mansions from Cliveden to Rainham. Commanding a bankside bluff in Buckinghamshire, Cliveden was designed by Charles Barry, the architect of the Palace of Westminster. With no surrounding agricultural estate, the mansion was built as a wealthy powerhouse for its spectacular riverside views, and is now famous for its heritage of twentieth-century political intrigue, whether stories of the so called pro-appeasement Cliveden Set or the Profumo Affair of the 1960s. Far off the beaten tourist track downstream in Essex, by the Thames Estuary, Rainham Hall now seems on the edge of things, but was in its time two centuries ago very much a commercial centre, the focal point of an extensive trading enterprise, and a witness to river trade and industry. Half-hidden in the midst of the industrial and motorway infrastructure surrounding Rainham Marshes, the Hall was ruinous at the time of the film in 1999 and 'Robinson thought he had discovered Dracula's house Carfax'. Now being restored, Rainham is haunted by a hidden history, for the story of the house is a story of London itself, its circulations and distributions, its comings and goings.

Below | Boat moored by the boat house on the River Thames at Cliveden, Buckinghamshire.

Trust
New Art

Many National Trust places were, in their day, meccas for the contemporary arts. Architects, designers and artists were commissioned by wealthy owners to turn their houses into beautiful exemplars of the latest fashions. The passing of time, however, all too easily diminishes the shock of the new. For this reason, the National Trust has worked with support from Arts Council England and the Heritage Lottery Fund to enable today's contemporary artists to respond to the landscapes and built heritage that the Trust now looks after. Some of the results are shown here; they help to reveal landscapes in a wholly new and sometimes startling light.

Above | *The Gathering/Yr Helfa* in 2014 was a walking performance exploring the annual cycle of sheep-farming, and the culmination of three years' observation of life at Hafod Y Llan, a working hill farm in Snowdonia. A mixture of installations, poetry, drama and music, the piece unfolded through a four-hour performance that traced a 6-kilometre route through the farm and the landscape.

Left | In *Bound*, part of the 'Tell it to the Trees' exhibition at Croft Castle, Herefordshire in 2009–10, Philippa Lawrence wrapped a dead oak tree in strips of heavy-duty red cotton drill. The act of wrapping up the tree bound its trunk and branches in a very obvious way, but also bound the artist closer to the tree in its landscape. The stark colour draws attention to the natural form of the tree, making its presence more strongly felt.

Above | Tony Plant looks down on one of his transient sand drawings at Bedruthan Steps beach, Cornwall. For Plant, 'Coastlines, and the memories associated with it, change shape daily. My paintings and whole beach drawings are a personal response to spending time at the cross-over between water, rock, sand, weather, memory and time.'

Right | Red Earth, the Brighton-based artistic partnership of Caitlin Easterby and Simon Pascoe, was invited to produce a work at Birling Gap, East Sussex in 2005 to mark the impact of coastal changes. As part of their 'Geograph' project, *Trace* was a chalk and flint line built by artists, rangers and participants between high and low tide that ran parallel to the existing cliff face, tracing a contour of where the cliff face once stood.

Above | As part of the 'House of Bling' exhibition at Tattershall Castle in Lincolnshire in 2009, artist and designer Linda Florence created a 50-metre carpet-drawing cut into the central lawn. The patterns were inspired by decorative forms on ceramic and glass uncovered during excavations at the site. The work's ephemeral nature is echoed in the passing of the shadows from the great tower, a reminder of the transitory nature of the power and authority of the building itself.

Right | In 2011 Red Earth explored the archaeology and ecology of the South Downs through site-specific installations, performance journeys and experiential walks. As part of their 'Chalk' project, *River* was a 90-metre avenue built on Harting Down, West Sussex from locally coppiced hazel and ash. *River* was inspired by the ancient deer hunt, prehistoric structures, and the glacial meltwater that formed the valley after the last ice age.

Chapter 2

Ancient Places

Previous page | Castlerigg Stone Circle, a megalithic circle of 38 stones, stands near Keswick in Cumbria. It was probably built around 3000BC.

Left | Mam Tor, the site of a Bronze Age and early Iron Age hill fort, provides one of the most dramatic viewpoints in the Peak District. It stretches north over the Edale Valley to Kinder Scout and the Derwent Moors.

Many in England are conscious that they are living in an old country, distinguished by the physical survivals from the past, whether medieval churches, Tudor palaces or half-timbered cottages. Those mindful of living in the larger, multinational state of Britain (a much more recent formation dating from the eighteenth century) may also be mindful of living in an even older country – an Ancient Britain distinguished by the remains of Roman villas and fortifications, and, more remotely still, by the stone circles and burial mounds of the Stone, Bronze and Iron Ages.

The past is all around us, continually recovered and restored. But it has also been fabricated and fashioned too: eighteenth-century country houses and their gardens were consciously designed as classical interventions in the landscape, sometimes borrowing from pre-existing historic features. The garden at Stourhead is a perfect illustration of this intermingling of old and new. As well as the antique-looking temples and grottoes built as part of the garden's design, it includes a functioning parish church and a medieval cross (a relic transposed from Bristol).

Right | The medieval Bristol High Cross, the local St Peter's church and the newly built Palladian Bridge in the grounds at Stourhead in Wiltshire highlight the eighteenth-century fashion for mingling the genuinely ancient and the fabricated antique.

All the time, the past is being made and remade, researched and restaged as the setting for daily life and as the filter for understanding and imagining our place in the world. Throughout Europe, particularly from the eighteenth century, landscapes have been conceived as part of the 'national heritage', for both its inhabitants and its visitors. In part, this has been because the power to collect, preserve, restore and interpret historic landscapes has rested with national agencies. However, it also reflects the way nation-builders have used the remains of the past to create national narratives, including myths of origin. Local narratives, too, draw on ideas of landscape: rural communities evoke ancestral memories of common rights and folk customs in their seasonal gatherings, re-using old sites and materials and staging ritual festivities. Ancient landmarks like legendary trees, burial mounds and river crossings become symbolic landmarks, part of the terrain where tradition is a history that is lived, a sense of the past in the present.

Right | The Temple of Apollo, situated on a hilltop at Stourhead, provides outstanding views across the lake.

Left | Aerial view of the Figsbury Ring in Wiltshire, an Iron Age hill fort with a smaller central, possibly Neolithic, enclosure.

The remote and recent past intersect when we see ancient sites through the lens of those amateur and professional photographers who have studied and appreciated the landscape for more than two centuries. Often, it is the very speed of progress that brings the past to light. Hence, it is through excavations for new construction that the life of the ancient past is often revealed. The continual rebuilding of central London turns up the successive layers of its past: the remains of the Roman city, the bankside prehistoric artefacts that indicate the role of the Thames as a sacred river, and more remotely still the fossil remains found in gravel pits showing that mammoth and bison once stalked the earth beneath what are now suburban streets. New image-making technologies – including aerial photography, remote sensing and geophysical survey – may reveal ancient patterns. In this way, modernity and antiquity can appear to be two sides of the same coin.

Ruins are a recurrent motif. Presented as they are, in more or less good repair, ruins such as abbeys and castles offer picturesque images. Others, such as the scattered stones of Avebury, are merely fragments to be put back together, assembled and reconstructed to present an image of the ancient stone circle as a whole. Ruins stand, but what do they stand for? They prompt thoughts both on the past and on the passing of time in the present.

Ruins have enjoyed a recent revival in the arts as a subject for investigating processes of landscape change, both natural and social. They act as warnings from the past or signs of

Left | Detail of a road sign showing lichen on Abingdon Road, Oxford from Patrick Keiller's film *Robinson in Ruins*, 2010.

recession in the present, such as images of demolished factories or abandoned terraced streets, which are perhaps beyond restoration. Patrick Keiller's film *Robinson in Ruins* took shape during the financial crisis of 2008. There are many forms and registers of ruin in the film: a derelict caravan, deserted village, gutted mansion, slighted castle and disused quarry, as well as the less picturesque ruinations from collapsing car sales and closed public spaces. All are placed in terms of wider, uneven material changes in which ruin in one place may be an integral part of enrichment elsewhere. The film also charts the duration of the natural world, alongside the history of the human world, the deep time of geological structures and the life span of humble plants – from primroses which can live up to fifty years, to lichens which can live to five thousand years, seen embedded in the letters of a road sign.

Above | Two of the standing stones that make up the henge at Avebury. The complex, which is made up of three concentric rings of stones enclosed by a huge circular bank and ditch, lies at the heart of a prehistoric landscape in Wiltshire that includes West Kennet Long Barrow and Silbury Hill.

Hengescape

Stonehenge is the most iconic ancient place in Britain and has inspired a long and continuing sense of wonder concerning its origins and purpose. Some have focused on the monument in isolation, despite how crowded the place is in reality. Recent changes at Stonehenge have removed one of the roads that formerly passed directly by it, and have changed the route of public access so that it now leads from a purpose-built visitor centre some distance away across a surrounding landscape marked by other prehistoric remains. The new access route and visitor centre serve both to showcase scholarly research on Stonehenge and to reinstate the drama of the visit.

The setting of Stonehenge enhances the feelings of the sublime evoked by it. Salisbury Plain is an unusually open, uncultivated expanse for southern England, and it attracted Romantic writers, artists and tourists, all drawn by its legends, superstitions and wild weather. Stonehenge was conventionally pictured on a barren heath in wild, stormy conditions, the pleasurable terror of the site enhanced by its reimagination as a site of primitive ritual and sacrifice. The antiquity and mystery of Salisbury Plain has, ironically, been deepened this century after being requisitioned as a military training ground. Aerial photographs from military aircraft first revealed the extent of prehistoric remains that are barely perceptible from the ground, and the exclusion of farming or settlement has meant that the site effectively functions as a sort of archaeological reserve.

There is still debate on the meaning and purpose of Stonehenge. For some, the monument had astronomical significance, its stones aligning accurately to the sun and other celestial bodies. For others, the henge was a theatre for sacred rituals so remote as to seem barely understandable. While seeking to uncover the original secrets of the stones, every age inevitably projects its own knowledge and values on the monument – and gets the Stonehenge it deserves or desires, as Jacquetta Hawkes so memorably observed. Over time the stones have been repositioned or straightened, actually or conjecturally, and variously linked to other sites in the immediate surroundings or further afield. The earliest historians of the monument speculated that it was built either by the Romans, or by the Ancient Britons they conquered, under a priestly

Right | J. W. M. Turner, *Stonehenge during a Storm*, c.1827, watercolour on paper, The Salisbury Museum.

Stonehenge, Wiltshire, 3 August 2013 by Simon Roberts.

class of Druids – speculations that were dependent on their particular views of civilisation and barbarism. Modern ideas and technologies of time (principally radio carbon analysis) now estimate that it was first built around 3,000BC, making it as old as the Pyramids, if not older.

New light continues to be shone on Stonehenge's origins. The pioneering surveys of ancient Wiltshire commissioned by aristocratic antiquarian Richard Colt Hoare, and launched from his library at Stourhead, have inspired more recent reinterpretations of the stones. Colt Hoare commissioned survey maps of Durrington Walls, a barely discernible embanked site two miles north-east of Stonehenge, on the banks of the river Avon. This was the site of one of the largest Neolithic settlements in North-West Somerset, a place where the living gathered and feasted before the procession, along ritual avenues, to Stonehenge.

It has long been known that Durrington Walls was constructed in wood, and the structures were probably trilithons. (A trilithon is made from two large vertical stones or posts supporting a third horizontally across it – as seen at Stonehenge.) But its relationship to Stonehenge may have been identified thanks to the brilliant flash of insight from a scholar visiting from Madagascar. On first seeing the site, he said its significance seemed obvious, for in the ancestral culture of his home island, wood was used to accommodate the living, and stone to house the dead. This scholarly reimagination may not have welcomed back the Druids, but there is nonetheless a renewed interest in priestly cults – perhaps reflecting a wider academic recognition of the power of religion in all periods and all places.

Stonehenge was built and used over a long period, some fifteen hundred years or more, and was from its beginnings a central iconic site within a wider geographical region. But it was not alone. Other prehistoric structures and shrines are being revealed as part of a sacred landscape. When novelist Thomas Hardy discovered an ancient burial in the foundations of his new house Max Gate outside Dorchester, he wasn't to know how it connected with the ancient Wessex

he evoked in his fiction, notably the scene set at Stonehenge in *Tess of the D'Urbervilles* (1891), the site of a sacrifice to mirror the heroine's own. In 1987 mechanical diggers, constructing a new bypass, revealed one half of a henge, now named Flagstonehenge, which still lies buried under the flagstones of Hardy's garden.

Richard Long's *Cerne Abbas Walk* (1975) is a key artwork in the revival of both landscape and antiquity in British art and culture during the 1970s. Richard Long expanded the field of fine art to take in a range of sites, spaces and practices, commemorating his journeys, largely on foot, with photographs, texts and inscribed maps, as combined in *Cerne Abbas Walk*. In works of this period, the artist focuses on the West Country, in a region extending from his childhood home in Bristol. He uses formal geometrical figures, lines, squares, rectangles, circles and spirals to frame stretches of country, as shown in photographs or on Ordnance Survey maps. Walking within or along these stretches, Long follows established topographical features, like riverbanks, or as far as possible, the lines themselves. The walks act as a form of excavation or transect, which reveal multiple layers of landscape history, from prehistory to the present, and inscribe new lines on the land in the spirit of older ones.

In the 1970s the wider region of chalk country framed by Long's square of map had been rediscovered as an ancient landscape. The remains of megaliths, burial mounds and fortifications impressed anew, along with such legendary hills as Glastonbury

Left | Glastonbury Tor is one of the most spiritual sites in the country. Topped by St Michael's Tower, it rises up over the Somerset Levels and looks out across Dorset, Wiltshire and Wales.

Right | The enigmatic head of the White Horse at Uffington, which gallops across the chalk downs in Oxfordshire. The figure is one of a number of ancient natural and man-made sites around White Horse Hill that have been the subject of legend and folklore, including the Manger, Dragon Hill and Uffington Castle.

Tor and Silbury Hill, and mysterious figures carved into the turf of chalk downs like the Cerne Abbas Giant. The Giant is 55 metres high and has long been a source of controversy, not only for its conspicuously erect phallus but for conflicting claims about its historical origins and purpose. Although now regarded by scholars as dating from the seventeenth century, a crude satire on Oliver Cromwell's heroic image as 'England's Hercules', the Giant was largely viewed in the 1970s as a pagan fertility figure, either Romano-British or Celtic. As an icon of English landscape, repeatedly used as a logo for advertising campaigns, the Cerne Giant has been continually reinterpreted. From time to time, too, it has literally been reinscribed into the landscape when recut, reshaped and recovered (as happened after the Second World War, when it had been concealed to avoid being used as a navigational tool by enemy aircraft).

Long's artwork, *Cerne Abbas Walk*, overlays a postcard, purchased in a local shop, showing an aerial photograph of the giant, on a section of the Ordnance Survey's one-inch map of the area. The Giant's figure is aligned on a north-south axis passing from the coast to the horizon of another photograph, taken by Long himself and described as 'the most typical and apt view of the landscape covered by the walk'. It is less a picturesque view than the kind of illustration found in geography books of the time, showing patterns of land forms and land use. The axis passes through the location where the Cerne Giant earthwork is located. Pivoting on this point, a circle encloses what the text at the top of the map states is 'A Six Day Walk Over all Roads, Lanes and Double Tracks inside a Six Mile Circle Centred on the Giant of Cerne Abbas'. The pattern of the walks inked on to the map recalls the mandala images popular at the time in hippie circles – part cosmic diagram, part cart wheel, echoing the double tracks made by the rims of cart wheels. The image is geomorphological as well as geometrical, the walking routes following the main north river valley of the Cerne and tributary dry valleys.

As a collage of various sites, made using different optics within the same field of vision, Long's *Cerne Abbas Walk* alludes to a longer visual culture of landscape archaeology. This includes popular speculative works issued a half century before by Alfred Watkins and his fringe archaeology followers, who made works of inscribed maps and photographs to connect a range of historic sites within networks of ancient British power and wider movements of pagan worship, including – to the shock of English current opinion – ancient priapic cults. The Cerne Abbas giant was given to the National Trust in 1920, restored and refashioned, the phallus lengthened by a third to what was formerly the navel. The only scheduled ancient monument to be subject to efforts to press a criminal charge of public indecency, the Giant was also the only full-frontal sexual image to be openly circulated as a greetings card by the General Post Office.

Below | Aerial view of the Cerne Abbas Giant in Dorset, whose age and meaning are continually reinterpreted.

Left | Richard Long, *Cerne Abbas Walk*, 1975, mixed media, Tate. The work is the result of a six-day walk in Dorset along roads, lanes and double tracks inside a 6-mile wide circle centred on the Giant.

A SIX DAY WALK OVER ALL ROADS, LANES AND DOUBLE TRACKS INSIDE
A SIX MILE WIDE CIRCLE CENTRED ON THE GIANT OF CERNE ABBAS.

DORSET 1975

Landscapes of Memory

The full history of a landscape is sometimes revealed only in the lie of the land. Iron Age and Bronze Age hill forts are dramatic examples of the imprint left in a landscape by past generations. Their continuing presence is a constant echo of our forebears and their world. The effect can be more subtle, too: on the beach at Formby, prehistoric footprints are occasionally revealed by the tide. In this way the landscape acts as a powerful aide-memoire, to remind us that we are not the first to have walked this terrain, and nor will we be the last.

Above | The Head Set at the Gold Mine has two trucks on the tracks for carrying away the spoil at Dolaucothi Gold Mines, Llanwrda, Carmarthenshire. The Romans mined for gold here, a practice that continued right into the nineteenth and twentieth centuries. The Dolaucothi Estate was given to the National Trust by the Johnes family in 1941.

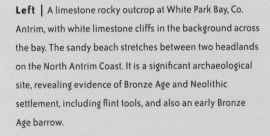

Left | A limestone rocky outcrop at White Park Bay, Co. Antrim, with white limestone cliffs in the background across the bay. The sandy beach stretches between two headlands on the North Antrim Coast. It is a significant archaeological site, revealing evidence of Bronze Age and Neolithic settlement, including flint tools, and also an early Bronze Age barrow.

Above | View of Hod Hill, Dorset, and the surrounding countryside. Now significant for being a vital calcareous grassland habitat, noted for its butterflies and wildflowers, Hod Hill was once an Iron Age hill fort, which was later captured and occupied by the Romans.

Above | Mam Tor in the Peak District of Derbyshire is also known as the Shivering Mountain because of the frequent landslips on its eastern face. At its summit is a late Bronze Age and early Iron Age hill fort.

Right | Examining prehistoric footprints on the beach at Formby Point, Merseyside. These tracks were made 7,500 years ago and were preserved by shifting sands and layers of silt. Coastal erosion today means successive layers of the prints are being revealed, and then almost as quickly lost to the tide. For Robert Macfarlane, author of *The Old Ways*, following these steps is like 'reading one of the earliest stories, told not in print but in footprint'.

Above | Sutton Hoo is sometimes referred to as Page 1 of English history. The burial site of an Anglo Saxon king, this place contains the origins of so much of what it means to be English: language, religion, custom, craft. The Saxon settlers chose to bury their king in a ship dragged to the top of a hill overlooking the Deben Estuary: the routeway to their homelands across the North Sea.

Below | The Iron Age hill fort at Badbury Rings in Dorset came to the National Trust when the Kingston Lacey Estate was acquired in the 1980s. Bronze Age burial mounds here speak to an even greater antiquity, while the whole area was settled by the Romans from the first to fifth centuries AD.

Wallscape

The major monument of Roman Britain is Hadrian's Wall, running coast to coast across the far north of England. It is 73 miles in length from the estuary of the Solway to the estuary of the Tyne, and crosses a range of scenes, from upland pasture to industrial towns. The Wall is a complex and challenging monument to maintain and manage, with more than 50 organisations and 700 private individuals owning particular sections. It is a requirement of the Wall's designation as a World Heritage Site that it is managed as a single entity along its length and for a 10-mile zone to either side, and that its historical significance is defined by a broad range of cultural values, accommodating the range of interests of those who conserve, use and enjoy the site, including the million or so people who live or work within the Wall's wider region.

The Wall is now understood as being more than a linear monument, one narrowly bounded in time and space, and is instead viewed from a broader perspective that encompasses the developing landscape of its immediate surroundings and its influence and legacy. This extends from the material remains of the monument during its three centuries of Roman occupation to the subsequent history of how those remains have been quarried to build houses, farms and roads. It also includes the many and complex ways the Wall has been interpreted, in images and texts, over its sixteen centuries since the end of Roman occupation. Reflecting changing views of Roman civilisation, and the effects of its empire, these interpretations have in turn shaped the landscape of the wall, both the repairs and restorations made to the fabric and its surroundings and the views created along its length. Here is a 'living wall', one that is continually reactivated.

A team from Durham University, led by Richard Hingley, has examined how the meaning of the Wall has been made and remade. Excavating an extensive range of sources, including the rich seam of factual and fictional writings on the wall, the team has also incorporated new ethnographic and observational fieldwork. The Wall has been variously represented and experienced – surveyed in maps, written on the page, re-created by models, featured in re-enactments, encoded in visitor conduct, inscribed in the earth by excavations, and set in stone in restorations and reconstructions. Running through a long-contested political border country, the Wall has been part of wider

Left | Hadrian's Wall stretches into the distance, following the line of north-facing cliffs formed by the outcrop of Whin Sill.

Above | Housesteads, one of 16 permanent bases on Hadrian's Wall, is the best preserved of all the forts along its length. Its original name 'Vercovicium' meant 'the place of effective fighters'.

debates about national and imperial identities. Different and competing views of what the Romans did for us have depended on geographical vantage point, on either side or either end of the Wall, as much as social perspective.

From Tudor times, the Wall was enlisted by British imperialists who saw themselves as inheritors of the mantle of ancient Rome. It was physically requisitioned in the mid-eighteenth century during the Jacobite uprisings in Scotland, to create a new infrastructure of fortification and military communication. Scottish observers have been more equivocal, some regarding the Wall as a sign of the resistance to Roman imperial aggression by the braveheart Celts, freedom fighters in contrast to the servile peoples to the south. In the nineteenth century, transportation improvements first made the monument a major tourist destination and the Wall's attribution to Hadrian was firmly established, and the growing industrial city of Newcastle to the east exercised a powerful influence on views of the Wall. By contrast, the view from the west, from Carlisle, has been less prominent. In 2003, the opening of the 84-mile coast to coast Hadrian's Wall National Trail, with new gates, stiles, signs and commemorative structures, has helped to illuminate the Wall's cultural significance.

At Housesteads, the National Trust owns the Fort as well as 5 miles of wall and more than a thousand hectares (2,470 acres) of land surrounding it, while English Heritage looks after the monument. Here Hadrian's Wall is presented to the visitor in its most iconic and dramatic form. In the classic vista, it snakes across wide open spaces, the impressive remains of its ramparts built on to the cliff-like geological exposure of Whin Sill. This sublime conjunction of culture and nature, ancient human and geographical history, is a centrepiece of the Northumberland National Park.

Right | Cattle grazing on pasture land near Hadrian's Wall in Northumberland.

Below | Whin Sill comes to an abrupt end at the Northumberland coast, and provided a strong defensive position for Dunstanburgh Castle.

The man originally responsible for creating the wallscape we see today at Housesteads was a leading light of Victorian Newcastle, John Clayton. As Town Clerk of the city, Clayton helped shape its modern civic architecture, and as a key figure in its Antiquarian Society, he shaped the landscape of the past. Initially concerned about the robbing of stones from the Wall, Clayton built up a private estate to preserve the remains – and then went much further, excavating, consolidating and rebuilding, and clearing away medieval structures and arable fields. Thus an impressive rampart wall, punctuated by forts, now stands among empty pastures, creating sweeping panoramic vistas for the viewer. The whole is an impressive project of antiquarian-style landscaping, in the tradition that mixes new parkland with restored ruins, and it was not long before this stretch was called the Clayton Wall.

We can understand more of how Victorians viewed the Wall in Wallington Hall, from the murals painted by Newcastle artist William Bell Scott for a house remodelled by Newcastle architect John Dobson. The scene of the mural called *Building the Roman Wall* is set to the west of Housesteads at Hotbank Crags and shows the partly constructed curtain wall under attack from the north by Caledonians. A Roman officer dominates a group of Ancient Britons who have downed tools to cook and gamble, while behind him, standing firm, are cohorts of Moors, Spaniards and Germans, part of the multi-ethnic make-up of the Roman army. A Moor holds a surveying instrument

in one hand and a shield in the other, his legionary dress indicating him to be a citizen of the empire. The picture demonstrates the widespread interest in the multicultural character of the Roman empire, but also acts as a mirror of Victorian Britain's concern about the military frontiers of its empire, and the degree to which recruiting native soldiers and mercenaries, serving close to their homelands, secured the borders – or indicated that Britain's imperium was dangerously overstretched. The Indian Mutiny would take place just one year after the mural was finished.

The building of Hadrian's Wall is the first in a sequence of scenes of Border History running around the enclosed courtyard of Wallington Hall, which ends with a mural showing the construction of nineteenth-century industrial Tyneside. This is a scene focused not on walls but bridges. Insolent-looking ancient Britons have been displaced in the course of civilization by skilled, hard-working modern Britons, loading coal, hammering ingots of iron, making locomotives, ships, guns and anchors. This Tyneside scene celebrates the work of local hero George Stephenson, the pioneer mechanical and civil engineer, and in particular the great railway viaducts he designed to help connect Scotland and England, and so build an integrated industrial nation state. A young child waits with her father's dinner, a schoolbook in her lap. A newspaper announces the

Above | Hadrian's Wall at Hotbank Crags, Northumberland.

Right | William Bell Scott, *Building the Roman Wall*, 1857, one of the murals in the Central Hall at Wallington, a 5,261-hectare (13,000-acre) estate near Morpeth in Northumberland.

ADRIANVS MVRVM DVXIT QVI BARBAROS ROMANOSQVE DIVIDERET.

Below | The enclosed courtyard at Wallington Hall, where the William Bell Scott murals are displayed.

victory of Garibaldi, an international hero of the liberal progressive views on display in the picture, which projects British global power and emphasises the productivity of manufacture, engineering and trade rather than the costs of colonial conquest.

As the name indicates, Wallsend was where Hadrian's Wall terminated. In Roman times, this was on the wild banks of the Tyne; now it is in the streets of a former shipyard district of the greater Tyneside conurbation. Here we seem a world away from Housesteads. Little remains of the Wall itself, though the local area has long been conscious of its presence, finding and sometimes relocating fragments, and marking out the ground plans of foundations. During the 1970s, large areas of housing were cleared for redevelopment, enabling extensive archaeological investigations that revealed almost the entire fort site. During the late 1990s, a multi-million pound cultural regeneration development included the building of a museum, Segedunum, and the reconstruction of a Roman bathhouse. Difficult to comprehend at ground level, the fort site is visible from the museum's viewing tower, some 35 metres high, along with a wider panorama of the locality's long landscape history, including former industrial areas. Consciously referencing Wallsend's shipbuilding heritage, the viewing tower takes the form of a ship's bridge, in a version of local heritage which twins classical and modern engineering achievements.

There is a renewed interest in the varied social and geographical population of the Wall's garrisons, as well as a revival of Victorian concerns with its civil as much as its military history, its mundane world as much as its monumental fabric. The occupation is seen less as a matter of Romans coming, seeing and conquering, and more a matter of Romans living and working, the army itself being its own community. Indeed the Wall ceases to be an exclusive place, and becomes more inclusive – a change that partly reflects contemporary social agendas about identity, diversity, citizenship, migration and cohesion. The Wall is now an element of the Frontiers of the Roman Empire World Heritage Site, within a world in which borders and border security are, as ever, a matter of political debate and dispute.

Recent exhibitions display the broader culture of the Wall community to the visiting public, including its domestic, everyday life – from the growing of food to rituals of religious observance, all displayed via a range of objects, original and replica, material and virtual, alongside newly commissioned artworks. These locate the Wall within a broader geography, its peoples drawn from the shores of Africa, the forests of Bavaria, the mountains of the Balkans and the plains of Iberia. This is a view of the Wall as a gathering place rather than a barrier, a site of contact and encounter, not just about keeping people out but about bringing people in. This view also finds a place for the varied religious practices tolerated by the army, renewing the attention paid by the Victorians to the shrines and votive objects they valued.

Left and below | The South Granary (left) and Latrines (below) at Housesteads Fort along Hadrian's Wall. Excavated remains of the barracks block, hospital, and Commander's House, can also be seen today. These, together with evidence of a parade ground and temple area, civilian settlement, cultivated fields and roads surrounding the fort, have made it possible to build up a broader picture of everyday life.

Ruins in the Landscape

Landscapes can signal a variety of time periods. Lancelot 'Capability' Brown was criticised in his day for his insensitive approach to past landscapes, since his designs often sought to erase traces of formal gardens, or even whole settlements. Another landscape tactic, however, was to embrace the past within the landscape, making a feature of historic relics and ruins. The aim sometimes was to create a deliberately picturesque effect, yet at the same time ruins – contrived or otherwise – can powerfully convey mood and meaning, as mementoes of our own mortality. National Trust sites frequently feature ruins as part of the wider landscape, held in a moment of arrested decay.

Above | The Temple of Friendship in the gardens at Stowe, Buckinghamshire, showing its arches, columns and ruined state, a result of a fire in the early nineteenth century. Designed by James Gibbs, the temple is dedicated to a group of opposition Whigs, and was completed in 1739.

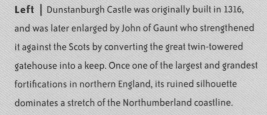

Left | Dunstanburgh Castle was originally built in 1316, and was later enlarged by John of Gaunt who strengthened it against the Scots by converting the great twin-towered gatehouse into a keep. Once one of the largest and grandest fortifications in northern England, its ruined silhouette dominates a stretch of the Northumberland coastline.

Above | The Tuscan columns on the arcaded side of the Orangery at Gibside, Newcastle-upon-Tyne. The Orangery was begun in 1772 to a design attributed to James Paine. Its ruined state echoes that of the hall itself, now an empty shell. Nonetheless, the property is a popular draw for local people.

Above | This is a purpose-built ruin, crowning a hill in the park at Wimpole Hall, Cambridgeshire. Commissioned by Philip Yorke, 1st Earl of Hardwicke, the design is by Sanderson Miller, a noted architect of picturesque follies and other contrivances in the landscape. The ruins eventually formed part of Capability Brown's design for Wimpole, serving as an eye-catching feature from the house. The folly has recently been restored for public access.

Left | The ruins of Corfe Castle in Dorset. The Castle dates to the eleventh century, and was further enlarged by King John and his successors. It was sold to the Bankes family in the seventeenth century, and came to the National Trust with the Kingston Lacy Estate in 1982. Corfe has been a ruin ever since the Civil War, when it was besieged and then demolished by Parliamentarian forces.

Above | The ruins of the house from the Main Lawn at Nymans, West Sussex. Nymans was purchased by Ludwig Messel in the late nineteenth century as a family home surrounded by a garden featuring plants from across the globe. The house was partially destroyed by fire in 1947, and only the north-east end rebuilt.

Spirit of Place

The Christian colonisation of Britain was a matter of converting places as well as people. The Church took over and adapted formerly pagan sites such as healing springs, mythical hills, haunted crossroads, and legendary trees, as well as building new structures – churches, cathedrals and abbeys, and the ecclesiastical geography of the parishes, dioceses and estates which supported them. Often the only stone buildings in a region, as well as being the tallest, medieval churches were major public landmarks, their towers and spires acting as beacons in the landscape. They were part of a wider devotional network of wayside shrines, stone crosses, holy wells, hermitages and pilgrim paths. This religiously reformed landscape did not entirely displace the ways of a much older world. The haunts of pagan belief and folk superstition, the ancient spirits of place, persisted for centuries, particularly in the countryside.

Such was the density of parish churches in eastern England – there were well over a thousand in Norfolk by 1600, more than the whole of Scotland – that any one view of this low-lying landscape would feature their towers, sited on small inclines or along ranges of hills. Running north from the cathedral city of Lincoln are a succession of regularly spaced parish churches along a limestone ridge, culminating in the village of Alkborough. The church at Alkborough overlooks the wide panorama of the Humber Estuary, of lands, rivers, sea and sky.

Like many early churches, Alkborough was built next to a spring, which may be the cultural source of its patron saint, John the Baptist. Its commanding position occupies an ancient settlement, with earthworks. The majestic tower, added in the tenth century, is in a style termed Romanesque because of its echo of the Roman Church, and includes masonry blocks from nearby Roman ruins framing local limestone quarried from the hills. The tower was built as both an entrance into the world, with the baptismal font at its base, and as an exit, coffins being placed there before burial. A bell chamber on its upper storey was constructed to create the plangent sounds for burial. The bells tolled over the burial ground below, but rang out much further, across the fields, and further still across the waters, creating a sacred soundscape. The role of bells in liturgy was to drive away demons and help blast the soul from purgatory to heaven, the soul figuring as a bird, like the birds lifting off from the estuary waters to soar into the overarching sky.

Left | The church tower rises up out of the
landscape in the hamlet of Glandford, north Norfolk.

Above | Julian's Bower at Alkborough in Lincolnshire. The turf labyrinth, which has been maintained over many centuries, lies on the summit of hills overlooking the Humber Estuary.

A short distance from the church at Alkborough is a labyrinth, named Julian's Bower, cut into the turf of a village green. Turf labyrinths are enigmatic features in the landscape, and fragile ones too, easily erased by agriculture or building development. Those that survive need to be continually recut lest they disappear due to erosion or overgrowth. The labyrinth at Alkborough has probably survived because it is located in a thinly populated rural region, and on common land in the village, and also because generations of villagers have valued it as an amenity. Local squires have appreciated it too, as an ornamental feature, a vantage point on a panoramic landscape and an historical relic.

Turf labyrinths were first recorded in writing in the seventeenth century, but are evidently much older. Initially they were assumed to be Roman, the former sites of martial games said to have been introduced into the empire by Julius, the son of Aeneas of Troy – a city with maze-like defensive walls. The few tourists who ventured this far north – on excursions from the Roman remains of Lincoln, following the modern road along the route of the Roman Ermine Street – looked upon Julian's Bower as part of a fortification. It was, after all, strategically set on the summit of hills overlooking the Humber Estuary, and could offer advance warning of attacks by an enemy fleet.

Few tourists seem to have registered surprise to find the labyrinth in such a state of high preservation despite the passing of so many centuries. The condition of Julian's Bower owed much to the efforts of the lord of the manor, Thomas Goulton, who as well as modernising his farms and waterways landscaped the entire hillside. A period of decay followed, but his successor John Goulton-Constable, a Fellow of the Society of Antiquaries, restored the labyrinth on the understanding that it was a medieval Christian relic. He argued that it was first constructed by twelfth-century Benedictine monks occupying a cell or grange in the village, an outlier of their main monastery at Spalding. He had a version cut into the porch floor of the parish church, as a template for returfing, which was modelled on the labyrinths in Continental churches and cathedrals – famously Chartres, whose labyrinth is almost identical in plan to that at Alkborough. These labyrinths are legible as a single spiritual pathway, winding through the four points of the earth's compass to Jerusalem as the world's geographical and spiritual centre, as shown in *mappae mundi*, maps of the medieval world picture. Julian's Bower also has a more terrestrial direction, its central axis aligned directly to the spire of York Minster.

Julian's Bower survived as a site of village games, with an air of ritual mystery. A Victorian gentleman recalled the pleasures of 'running it in and out', in company with others early in the nineteenth century, of seeing the villagers playing May-eve games about it, 'under an indefinite persuasion of something unseen and unknown co-operating with them'. These recollections are perhaps tinctured by a literary as well as personal memory. The Fairy Queen Titania's account of a 'mazed world' in Shakespeare's *A Midsummer Night's Dream* is of a land overtaken by a flood, such that 'quaint mazes in the wanton green / For lack of tread are indistinguishable'.

Recently restored by English Heritage with hardy turf used for professional soccer pitches, Julian's Bower is a good place to ponder the imaginative power of labyrinths. Still echoing the wide-ranging confluence of waterways it overlooks, even in today's less meandering channels, it supports speculations that 'contemplating the course of rivers' was a primordial source for the idea of the labyrinth. The site forms one of the excursions from Hibaldstow, the home village of performance artist Mike Pearson. In his 'guide book through a landscape imagined' *In Comes I* (2007), Julian's Bower acts as a diagram to map millennia of history, winding backwards to the great flood of a remote past (a post-glacial inundation that created a vast meltwater lake) and forwards to a recent scheme to deal with rising sea levels, which has allowed existing flood defences to be breached so that the waters of the estuary can spread again.

The sacred realm of Catholic devotional sites and folk custom was not entirely displaced by the reforming zeal of Protestant reformers. The source of sanctification shifted with the Reformation from place to people: from something inherent in the landscape to the

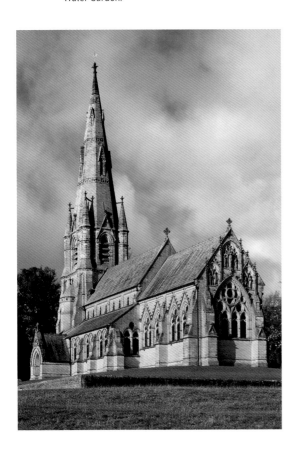

Below | St Mary's church, designed in the Gothic style by William Burges for the 1st Marquess and Marchioness of Ripon on the estate at Studley Royal Water Garden.

Left | A view along the River Skell towards Fountains Abbey, in North Yorkshire, which was home to a Cistercian community of monks from the twelfth century until the Dissolution in 1539.

thoughts and actions of those who lived and worked it. Theologically this represented a change from the sacred to the spiritual. The effect was to remodel, not dissolve, the devotional landscape, redistributing the realm of enchantment.

The simplicity, whitewashed walls and clear glass windows of reformed churches were believed to transmit and reflect the light of scriptural revelation. The challenge to traditional Anglicanism by dissenting congregations, including the brief period of state power held during the Puritan Commonwealth, was too radical a reform for some. There were pockets of resistance. The church at Staunton Harold in Leicestershire was built by a royalist landlord in his park during the Puritan Commonwealth, a hostile world that included most of his surrounding tenants. It was built in the Gothic style, its richly iconographic ceiling showing the skies of the Creation, and the inscription above the church entrance reading 'Ye Best Things in Ye Worst Times'.

Catholics continued, covertly, to frequent the remains of religious houses and shrines, viewing them as sacred reliquaries. These included the Lady Chapel and Holy Well at Mount Grace Priory at the foot of the Yorkshire Moors, and the abbey and church at Glastonbury Tor, which Joseph of Arimathea is said to have visited. For reforming

Protestants such ruins were triumphs in the war on religious corruption, part of the demolition of a profane world. The Reformation suited the secular powers that benefited from the breaking of papal authority, notably the aristocrats favoured with the spoils of formerly monastic lands. Some incorporated the ruins of abbeys within their new mansions and parks, lending them a poetic, antique aura that has persisted to the present.

The magnificent remains of Fountains Abbey, Yorkshire enshrine an eighteenth-century landscape garden, Studley Royal, which is now a World Heritage Site. Generations of estate owners kept the ruins in repair as an ornamental landmark, but the Victorian Marquess of Ripon, a pious Anglo-Catholic, venerated them more highly. He commissioned a sumptuous church, built in medieval Gothic style, in another part of the park. The Abbey ruins are now valued as a spiritual site, with occasional services in

Left | The Gothic stone steps on the west front of Lacock Abbey. The abbey underwent a series of alterations in the Gothic Revivial style under the ownership of John Ivory Talbot.

Above | Lacock Abbey, in Wiltshire, seen across the River Avon. The original abbey was converted into a house by Sir William Sharington from 1539 with the demolition of the church. The octagonal tower was built in 1550.

the cloisters and clergy on hand to visitors to dispense pastoral advice. In the tradition of romantically mantled ruins, Fountains Abbey is also esteemed as a richly ecological site, for its many varieties of bat as well as wall flora.

At Lacock Abbey, Wiltshire the cloisters of the former nunnery were incorporated into the fabric of a new house, with harmonising additions in the style of Gothic Revival. Lacock Abbey's most famous owner, the pioneering photographer Henry Fox Talbot, used the antique style architecture to facilitate the most modern form of picture making, as well as to evoke the ghosts of the past, which he described as 'the holy sisterhood pacing in silent meditation'. In early photography it seemed that physical sites and processes were themselves 'the pencil of nature' creating these images; Lacock Abbey was the first building, Fox Talbot announced to the Royal Society in 1839, 'that was ever known to have drawn its own picture'.

In Protestant culture, Anglican or Puritan, the English landscape was imagined in terms of the Bible, through the temples, pastures and gardens of the Old and New Testaments. Heaths and barren hills stood in for deserts, extreme storms and tides for great floods. Nature was still seen as God's Book, in which His authority was manifested. In this way the landscape was a joint creation, crafted by God and completed by Man, toiling industriously. Of course, there were still many sinful places in this landscape, in cities or wildernesses, to tempt those making their way in the world and to deflect them from the straight and narrow path of righteousness.

Thus many nineteenth-century paintings of the countryside were forms of religious art, of a down-to-earth kind. Sanctity for some artists resided in antiquity, in the very survival of sites, consecrated by continued reverence or customary use. Others were drawn to the sublime terror of wilder nature, to the residual superstition of the many crags, cliffs and caves assigned to the Devil or to Giants. Romantic nature worship offered sacred landscape for those less scriptural in their thoughts, even before the effect of scientific understanding posed a challenge to Biblical authority. The very deepening awareness of time and space came as a revelation of a kind, a sublime awakening to a new world of wonders.

Left | The North Cloister walk, at Lacock Abbey. The cloisters, sacristy, chapter house and monastic rooms all survived the abbey's conversion to the new house.

Temples of Delight

Religious buildings – churches, chapels, monasteries, temples – are among the most recognisable features in our landscape. Towers, steeples and spires can dominate a landscape for miles around, as indeed was the intention. A place of worship can be a welcoming sight, a place for communal gathering. It can also be a statement of power, designed to put people in their place – either by excluding them altogether or by segregating them by pew or box. In many National Trust places, churches and chapels have been integrated seamlessly into the landscape, signalling the marriage of the spiritual and the secular.

Above | View of St Peter's church, which overlooks the gardens at Stourhead, Wiltshire. The church is likely to date from the thirteenth century. It was significantly renovated by Henry Hoare, whose son was responsible for the famous landscape at Stourhead.

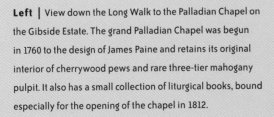

Left | View down the Long Walk to the Palladian Chapel on the Gibside Estate. The grand Palladian Chapel was begun in 1760 to the design of James Paine and retains its original interior of cherrywood pews and rare three-tier mahogany pulpit. It also has a small collection of liturgical books, bound especially for the opening of the chapel in 1812.

Above | The ruins of St Patrick's Chapel at Heysham Head. Like other early British Christian sites, the chapel was located close to the sea. Heysham Head is the most prominent cliff top in Lancashire, providing a dramatic backdrop to the ruins. The foreground shows two of the trench graves that are cut into a single slab rock, which date from the eleventh century and are unique in Britain.

Left | The spire of the Victorian Gothic chapel, seen over the serpentine lake at Clumber Park, Nottinghamshire. A chapel here was commissioned in 1864 by Henry Pelham-Clinton, 5th Duke of Newcastle, but remained uncompleted. It was subsequently demolished and a new chapel was built on the site to a design by G. F. Bodley, completed in 1889.

Left | The ruins of Hailes Abbey, Gloucestershire. A Cistercian abbey, founded in 1246 by Richard of Cornwall and dissolved Christmas Eve 1539, Hailes never housed large numbers of monks but had extensive and elaborate buildings. It was financed by pilgrims visiting its renowned relic, 'the Holy Blood of Hailes' – allegedly a phial of Christ's blood.

Below | Croome d'Abitot, St Mary Magdalene church at Croome Park, Worcestershire, designed by Capability Brown with interiors by Robert Adam. According to Pevsner, it is 'one of the most serious of the Early Gothic Revival outside, one of the most elegant inside'. St Mary Magdalene church is owned by the Churches Conservation Trust.

Above | The east end and chancel from the nave at Staunton Harold, Leicestershire. The church was built in 1653, during the time of Oliver Cromwell's Commonwealth. It was commissioned by Sir Robert Shirley. Inside, the pews and wood panelling are made from local oak by the Melbourne joiner William Smith.

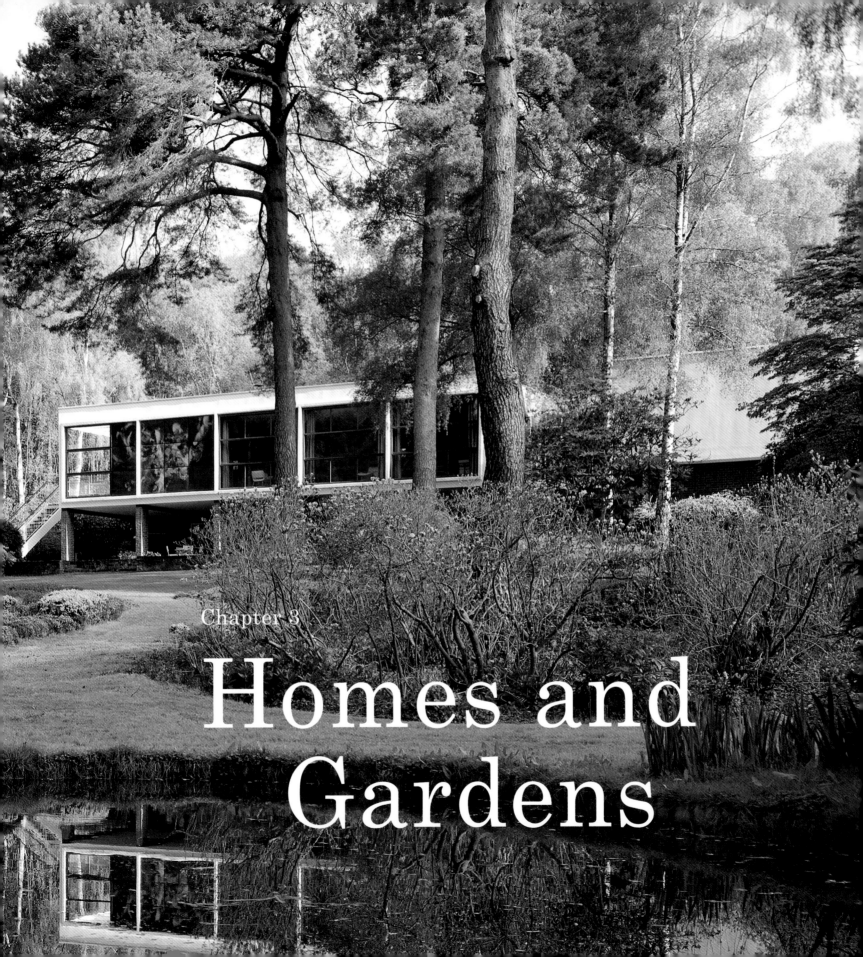

Chapter 3

Homes and Gardens

The idea of a landscape as a pleasing prospect owes a great deal to its origins in the domestic setting of houses, gardens and landed estates. The National Trust owns and cares for many such landscapes in all shapes and sizes, from palatial mansions in rolling acres to smaller villas and their grounds. As well as country houses, the Trust now manages dwellings that include servants' quarters, country cottages, suburban semis and urban back-to-backs.

The centrality of homes and gardens to landscape tastes is a rather complex matter. The domestic ideal for many people in Britain is to live in a house with a garden. Despite pressures for development, for infill and paving, domestic gardens take up more than 13 per cent of land in towns and cities. These private amenities are valued as habitats and routeways for wildlife. Along with public parks they illustrate the prevalence of the garden-city ideal, far beyond the places that were expressly designed in this way. The garden-city movement was an approach to urban planning dating from the turn of the twentieth century, when figures such as Ebenezer Howard advocated a blend of new housing with ample green space, including gardens.

Visitors to country houses are often keen to see examples of 'how the other half lived', whether downstairs or upstairs. Home truths, the verities of domestic life, persist in a variety of settings. So too do ground truths, the seasonal rounds of gardening, from digging to weeding. The past is brought home for a modern public in the excavations of ancient landscapes which reveal traces of domestic life, whether the layouts of prehistoric houses and hearths or the traces of familiar plants and garden plans in Roman villas. Participants can imaginatively situate themselves in such places, even if those past cultures entertained very different notions of what constitutes domestic

Above | A scarecrow watches over the vegetable garden at Calke Abbey in Derbyshire. Dating from the eighteenth century, the Physic Garden has grown herbs and exotic fruits, including pineapples, and continues to grow a variety of seasonal produce and soft fruits today.

space. In this way, homes and gardens become strange as well as familiar – in relation to themselves and to their wider worlds, in the recent as well as the remote past.

There is something mythical as well as material about homes and gardens. The domestic landscape, at whatever scale, has long been a complex one, with a wider resonance. We speak of the virtues of 'homelands' and of the 'home-made', and of garden cities and garden suburbs. Cultivated countryside is often described as being 'garden-like', and whole regions and nations are cast as domestic landscapes: Kent has long been the Garden of England, for example. In this way, England itself is imagined as a garden and the nation as a people of gardeners – a view that was mobilised during the Second World War by the Dig for Victory campaign. These images themselves draw on older and wider mythologies – biblical gardens, gardens of childhood and love, gardens of mourning and remembrance. As the devotional poem puts it – which can often be found on ornaments available in garden centres – we are 'closer to God in a Garden than anywhere else on earth'.

There is a powerful art and literature of homes and gardens, as comforting refuges from a wider world, a way of framing the world at large as a pleasing place. But in such works gardens may also have a dark side, and turn out to be strange, troubling places. Homes and gardens may be good things, bright and beautiful – but, like the Garden of Eden, they may also harbour serpents at the same time as they are bedecked with

Right | The Grade II listed conservatory at Sunnycroft, the Victorian surburban villa on the outskirts of Wellington in Shropshire.

Below | The familiar face of Peter Rabbit, who appeared in Beatrix Potter's *The Tale of Peter Rabbit* in 1902.

trees and flowers. The expulsion from Eden, for a life of labour not leisure, reminds us that gardens out there in the real world are places of hard work. The control and management of gardens in this way becomes critical to their very definition, fencing out people and nature as well as fencing them in.

Beatrix Potter's illustrated books for children draw on a powerful cult of cottages and gardens at the turn of the century. The stories explore some traditional, class-edged, rural tales about the security of hearth and home and the risks of the wider world – including trespassing in other people's gardens. In *The Tale of Peter Rabbit*, the reader explores a neat, productive vegetable garden, its cucumber frames, rows of plants and potting shed – all shown from ground level, and the perspective of a small child, its risks and rewards defined in terms of a family of rabbits. The family claim their customary share of the produce for their cosy, cottage-like burrow in the roots of a tree, and their stores include some of Mr McGregor's onions and carrots as well as herbs and blackberries, food for free foraged from the hedgerows.

The making and meaning of even modest gardens is important to their owners. This is just one finding of recent research by Andrew Church and colleagues at Brighton University, drawing on the Mass Observation Archive of everyday life begun in 1937. Gardens are places where ordinary people can create enchantment in commonplace surroundings, through the seasonal tasks – labours of love, even – of digging and weeding. Gardens also tell longer-term stories, documented in diaries and family photographs. These stories are personal but follow familiar plot lines of family life. Photographs show the seasonal and generational changes to gardens simply because they form the settings for family snaps: children playing on the lawn, couples cuddling by the flower bed, cats prowling the walls, grandparents dozing in deck chairs. With or without the design advice of makeover magazines and television programmes, gardens become the stage sets for the theatre of family life. And such photographs are a vernacular version of the more formal, aristocratic portraits set in landscape parks, paintings celebrating dynastic marriages and comings of age, or the outdoor pursuits of promenading, angling, music-making and admiring the view.

The cult of home and gardens is also a matter of conservation, a reaction to the spectre of their ruin, the prospect of gutted mansions and overgrown parks, abandoned villages and demolished cottages. The movement to preserve aristocratic landscapes in the mid-twentieth century was mobilised by images of decaying and dilapidated stately homes, a patrician heritage in danger in a post-war world of new money and financial accountability, of pop culture and new voices. Ironically, the aristocracy has by and large been remarkably successful in consolidating and expanding their power and influence, and some of the most visited stately homes and estates are still owned by long-standing titled families.

In some places, ruined country houses are part of a new more accessible landscape and, like ruins in ancient landscapes everywhere, become relics that may be imaginatively reassembled to create worlds of the past. The original mansion of Clumber Park, Nottinghamshire was demolished in 1938, but its surviving pleasure grounds, walled kitchen garden, glasshouses and stable yard, as well as an extensive wooded landscape park, are fragments that enable us to reimagine an aristocratic past. The latest country house acquisition of the Trust is a partially ruined mansion in Northumberland: the central block of Seaton Delaval was gutted by fire in 1822, a century after its building. Its architect John Vanbrugh was an early devotee of ruined mansions, and was keen to see the Gothic remains of Woodstock Manor conserved when he rebuilt Blenheim, even if he may not have imagined his own work suffering the same fate.

Such mansion ruins acquired a cultural value of their own, as sites for artistic inspiration and for philosophical contemplation of the passing of time and prospects for the future. Plans for Seaton Delaval, which have included extensive public consultation,

Above | *CO₂morrow*, the art project by Marcos Lutyens and Alessandro Marianantoni in the grounds of Seaton Delaval Hall. Commissioned by the National Trust in relation to concerns over conservation and climate change, the carbon-fibre installation shows changing levels of CO_2 in the atmosphere using data from readers at several Trust properties to illuminate LEDs within the sculpture.

have been similarly inspired, prompted to move beyond the walled world of country-house curatorship and to show the place of the estate in a longer history and wider world, including seafaring and industrialisation. Here, and also at Clumber, traditions of landscaping have been updated, with new commissions of contemporary art and design, outdoor installations and sculpture.

The comforting appeal of cottages and villages is made all the more piquant by images of 'the deserted village', abandoned through plague or by forced eviction, whether at the hands of landlords enclosing the landscape for parks, the military requisitioning it for training grounds, or as a result of redevelopment of various kinds. The village of Tyneham in Dorset was requisitioned by the army during the Second World War, as part of the Lulworth firing range, and is still part of the military estate. It is now a series of ruined buildings overgrown by gardens gone wild. Campaigns for the resettlement of the village, restored to its former state, have lapsed now that most of its original residents have died. The ruins of the village have been 'stabilised', tidied and made safe for tourists to visit on non-firing weekends, with the added amenities of car park, public conveniences, picnic tables and interpretative signs. Visitors find a time capsule, a ghost village spared the developments of post-war England, with an enviable position above the country's scenic heritage shoreline, the Jurassic Coast. Its picturesque appeal is further enhanced by being managed as a sanctuary for wildlife – an indication of the 'greening' of the military presence.

The National Trust owns two different kinds of picturesque estate settlement. Designed by John Nash, Blaise Hamlet in Gloucestershire is valued for its ornamental

Right | A traditional stone cottage on the High Street in Lacock village, near Chippenham. The estate of Lacock, including the Abbey and village, was given to the Trust in 1944 by Matilda Talbot.

Below | One of the cottages at Blaise Hamlet designed by John Nash in 1809 to house the Blaise Estate pensioners.

Above | The corner of 50–54 Inge Street and 55-63 Hurst Street, the Victorian back-to-backs in Birmingham.

Right | View of the communal courtyard of the back-to-backs, which was shared between about 15 families.

Left | The wash house, which opens on to the courtyard of the back-to-backs. This set-up of communal living arrangements was typical for many working-class people in the industrial cities.

gingerbread-style thatched cottages grouped around a village green, planned as much for its scenic attraction as for the comfort and convenience of the inhabitants. Laycock, Wiltshire is an inhabited place seemingly preserved in time. A once-flourishing industrial small town, it suffered a sudden decline when bypassed by the railway, but under estate ownership continued with its fabric intact. Now, with strict attention to its original appearance, Lacock is the outdoor stage set of choice for television and film costume dramas set in the eighteenth and nineteenth centuries.

The shadow side of these picturesque settlements is a more recently acquired National Trust property of Victorian back-to-backs. 55–63 Hurst Street/50–54 Inge Street, Birmingham is a nineteenth-century courtyard of working-class houses. Thousands of houses were built in this formation for the expanding population of Britain's industrial towns and cities, and at one time a quarter of Birmingham's residents lived in such homes. The houses have now been restored to reflect various periods between the 1840s and the 1970s. Workshops were originally built into the courtyard complex, enabling a large number of trades, most with links to the city's metal industry. Early residents made prams, bicycles, horse brasses, watch cases, locks and clock hands. Later residents manufactured glass eyes and set up shops. Around 15 families shared communal lavatories within the central courtyard, which was also used for washing and storing rubbish. This often led to squalid conditions (themselves intensified by industrial pollution) and there were inevitable conflicts. Indeed, it was the problems of the back-to-back housing model that paved the way for garden cities and ideal industrial villages like Bournville, on the outskirts of Birmingham. And yet, for all their material and social shortcomings, this arrangement also forged a sense of community and collective spirit. Today the back-to-backs are valued as amenities, and three houses are now available as 'holiday cottages'.

Water and the Country Garden

The juxtaposition of land and water is most strikingly observed on the coast. But water is also often deployed in landscape gardens, the calm glass-like surfaces of lakes and moats as a contrast to close-cropped grass. Gardens depend on water too, and the ornamental use of water in a garden often belies complex systems of irrigation. Water is now one of the most pressing issues facing many historic gardens, whether in terms of excess (such as flooding) or its lack (drought). Landscape scenes involving water are all the more valued at a time when gardeners are having to find ways to minimise its use.

Above | The hall from the lake at Blickling Estate, Norfolk. Blickling is a Jacobean mansion and was one of the first houses to be bequeathed to the Trust by the Country Houses Scheme through the will of Philip Kerr, Lord Lothian, who died in 1940.

Above | The stables and clockhouse at Dunham Massey, Cheshire. The River Bollin feeds the moat at the house, which is now a busy tourist attraction for the Greater Manchester area. Many of the buildings are listed and date from the eighteenth century. The house was used as a military hospital during the First World War.

Right | A *Liriodendron tulipifera* (tulip tree) on an island in the lake at Stourhead. Henry Hoare II ('the Magnificent') dammed a stream to create the lake in the middle of the eighteenth century. There are many tulip trees at Stourhead. They turn a butter-like colour in autumn and have a distinctive leaf shape.

Left | The Oxford Bridge at Stowe, Buckinghamshire. The bridge was built in 1761 and carries the Oxford Avenue from the south west. The stone urns feature decorative faces, emphasising the way the design combines both classical influences and more picturesque elements.

Above | The south front and lower lake at Ightham Mote, Kent. A Grade I-listed structure, for Pevsner this was 'the most complete small medieval manor house in the country'. Subsequent landscaping made much use of the medieval fish ponds to enhance the setting of the building.

Left | View from top of the grass amphitheatre at Claremont Landscape Garden, Surrey. The amphitheatre was created around 1722 by Charles Bridgeman and restored by the National Trust.

Above | View of The Cascade into the lake, showing rusticated columns and pavilions on the dam, in the garden at Studley Royal, North Yorkshire. The garden was the vision of John Aislabie and his son William. Their efforts turned land in the valley of the River Skell into one of England's most spectacular Georgian water gardens.

Right | View over the moat of the south range of Oxburgh Hall, Norfolk. Sir Edmund Bedingfeld built Oxburgh Hall in about 1482. The moat is fed by the River Gadder, and recent investment in the infrastructure and riverbanks here has helped to sustain the water levels in the moat. This has conservation benefits for both the building and wildlife.

Treasure Houses

Left | The Grand Staircase at Petworth House, showing the mural by Louis Laguerre of the Duchess of Somerset. The house contains the National Trust's finest collection of pictures with numerous works by Turner, Van Dyck, Reynolds and Blake.

Transferred to the National Trust in 1947, the palatial Petworth House and its park of 280 hectares (700 acres) exemplified the glamorous cult of the country house for a mid-twentieth century audience. The family continued to live in the mansion, with its fine collection of paintings and sculpture, and though shorn of its wider estate – which includes the town – Petworth House enjoyed its new status as a work of art, rather than the traditional status of a country house as a social and political centre. Here was a treasure house, not a powerhouse.

Petworth is staged to display developments commissioned by successive Earls of Egremont: a Baroque late seventeenth-century mansion, a mid-eighteenth-century landscaped park, and an early nineteenth-century art collection. Moreover, this was not a place that exhibited as many overseas interests and acquisitions as found in other great houses, including classical antiquities and old-master paintings; Petworth instead exhibited masterpieces of British art. Its park was designed by Lancelot Capability Brown, its art collection is dominated by works by J. M. W. Turner and includes many pictures of the house and park.

The set of Turner paintings commissioned for the Carved Room, overlooking the park, explore the range of estate and family interests at the height of Petworth's power in the early nineteenth century. Turner's paintings for landed patrons invariably represent their estates as working countryside, purposefully prosperous, the parkland shown as

Right | The four paintings by J. M. W. Turner restored to the panelling of the Carved Room at Petworth House. In total, there are 20 Turner paintings at Petworth.

The Petworth Park 10k, Petworth House, West Sussex, 21 May 2014 by Simon Roberts.

productive, grazed by livestock and planted with timber, and its outlying areas farmed and quarried. At Petworth, Turner went much further. His patron, the 3rd Earl of Egremont, turned the mansion into an artistic open house for the most modern artists of his day, and Turner himself was given a studio, encouraged to stay weeks at a time. Egremont was an advanced estate owner, practising the most progressive forms of agriculture and social development, and investing his money in commercial schemes to mobilise the riches of the entire region. Turner therefore chose to show how Capability Brown transformed the parkland into a panoramic vision of this new order: on one side a model farm takes over much of the deer park, and is grazed by sleek Southdown Sheep and plump pedigree pigs; on the other side a village cricket match is an example of his patron's local benevolence. An otherwise vast park, too empty and unsociable looking for tastes at the time, is filled in these pictures with domestic details and incident, looking more 'garden-like' to its admirers.

Two other Turner panoramas range more widely, well beyond the park, projecting his patron's enlightened interests. A view of the Chichester Canal, one of Egremont's investments, is plied by a three-master seagoing ship. Brighton, the fastest growing English town of the time, is viewed from the sea and shows the new iron pier for docking vessels. Turner's radiant, highly modern pictures were installed in a seemingly traditional setting: a room decorated with the seventeenth-century limewood carvings of another English master, Grinling Gibbons, and portraits of Egremont ancestors. Here guests from the far quarters of this highly informal, bohemian open house for artists and mistresses gathered each summer evening for dinner, to look both at the paintings on the wall and the views through the windows over the rolling acres of the estate.

The landscape gardener Humphry Repton was sometimes called upon by aristocratic patrons to modify landscapes in the grand style of Capability Brown, to make these places picturesquely domestic, more garden-like. Repton was more successful in establishing his own art of landscape by working at this modest scale on smaller estates, for lesser gentry, to design, or improve, pleasure grounds and houses for country squires or villa owners.

Repton's designs are highly theatrical. His so-called Red Books of plans use a trademark style of 'before' and 'after' views, removing an overlay of the dull scene that clients actually saw, to reveal the delightful scene the designer envisaged. Dramatic transformations, he showed, could be effected with relatively small adjustments – removing a fence, rerouting a road, trimming some trees – and not necessarily through major earthworks or dislocations. Repton's masterpiece is Sheringham Park, Norfolk, purchased by the National Trust in 1986, one of the few places where his design was fully realised on the ground and can still be seen today. Made from a small farming estate, this was a naturally scenographic landscape, an amphitheatre with vistas out over the countryside and the coast. It needed only a well-placed house and some modest modifications to enhance its social and aesthetic value and to reveal what Repton described as 'the treasures of Sheringham'. The acquisition of Sheringham came at a moment of change for National Trust, when its purpose was moving away from preserving country houses to offering public access to the countryside. Happily, Repton's original design for the landscape, which remains a management plan, was public-spirited, permitting a degree of access and emphasising the park's connections to the wider world.

Repton took a close interest in the landscape of Sheringham well before he produced his Red Book of designs in 1812, which helps to explain why it proved such an important and personal commission for him. It was, he said in his Red Book of designs, 'my most favourite work'. Before his career as a landscape gardener, he was a textile merchant in Norwich, and after taking early retirement he lived nearby at Sustead, among family and friends. In a guidebook he described this fertile and appealingly varied countryside – including farmland, small villages, old churches, pleasure grounds and woods – as 'The Garden of Norfolk'. When he was commissioned years later, in 1812, towards the end of his career, he pronounced that Sheringham had more 'natural beauty and local advantages' than 'any place I have ever seen'. The commission was a homecoming for Repton personally as much as an opportunity to design a new home for Abbot and Charlotte Upcher, young clients who shared his vision.

Repton's designs for Sheringham are a sign of the times. The year 1812 was eventful on the wider national and international stage. Britain was at war with France, and the threat of invasion was very real, coastal locations like Sheringham being particularly vulnerable. The country was wracked with social and financial troubles, including protests about the introduction of new textile machinery, the depression of working conditions and the treatment of an increasingly impoverished labour force. In April 1812, Repton told his son William 'the times look portentious ... all the country seems in Arms'. While Repton was relieved Sheringham lay beyond the textile region of Norfolk and the political influence of its workers, the spectre of social unrest explains his concerns for those who worked the land locally and their hardships. Repton's views echoe wider moral concerns. He wrote in the designs: 'Whether the poor slave be driven

Above | A design from Humphry Repton's 1812 Red Book for Sheringham, revealing the proposed new house from 'the turn' in the drive. Repton's clients Abbot and Charlotte Upcher are shown admiring the view, and Repton himself is shown sketching. Watercolour on paper, National Trust, on loan to the Royal Institute of British Architects.

Left | Design for entrance lodge from Repton's
Red Book for Sheringham. The road sign shows the
connections of the estate to neighbouring towns.

Left | The approach to Sheringham Hall. To shield the house from the North Sea winds, Repton chose a south-facing site protected by a wooded hillside.

Above | The temple at Sheringham Park was part of Repton's original designs, but was not built until 1975.

by the lash of the whip, or the dread o confinement in a work house, he must feel that men are not all equal altho' he may be taught to read that they are so.'

Despite, or perhaps because of, the dramatically shifting world of the time, 1812 proved a landmark year for landscape as a form of art and knowledge, for painting, design and for works of literature and science. The scope of the landscape arts, including Repton's designs, expanded to encompass a range of matters – the long ago and the far away, the distance of antiquity and the global reach of empire – the cultural imagination now extending to the very ends of the earth. An appreciation of landscape also became more socially extensive, more public, less the preserve of the rich and highly educated. Sites and scenery became more accessible to the middle classes, through travel and affordable prints, maps, books and scenographic entertainments.

The designs for Sheringham were Repton's most wide-ranging, most deeply thought and felt, a comprehensive scenic and social programme. They reflected both his anxieties about the period and his affection for the place. He was deeply concerned about the social and financial state of the nation and county, and also had his own personal insecurities about money and infirmity (following a recent carriage accident), but he was confident that his clients Abbot and Charlotte Upcher, socially conscientious Christians, would faithfully carry out his designs.

The new house, the pivot of the landscape design, was planned in collaboration with Repton's architect son John Adey. It was built in a fashionable Neo-classical style, with the air of a seaside villa. The house was designed for sociability as well as scenery, with rooms that were designed for music making and reading but which also opened up to the park and pleasure ground. Attention was paid to the fixtures and fittings; windows, mirrors, drapes, lamps and stained glass were all designed to frame and enhance the view, and to let the landscape in. The landscape took in the estate as a whole, the farming and fishing villages of Sheringham and a range of scenes – woodland, pasture, farmland and coast. Repton and his clients were also mindful of the connections to a wider world, by road to the rest of Norfolk and by sea to London and northern England. And they were focused on the social connections of Sheringham, promoting measures to improve and oversee relations between rich and poor, and secure the loyalty and affection of the local population at a time of national emergency.

Repton deployed a remarkable range of knowledge and feeling in his designs for Sheringham. The plans are both practical and poetic, about substance as well as spectacle, down to earth and highly flown. So landscape gardening at Sheringham

Below | View from the Gazebo across farmland towards the Weybourne Windmill and the coast.

encompassed a range of features. It incorporated the making of pleasure grounds around the house, with flower beds and greenhouses for exotics, sheltered from the chilly winds of the North Sea, and a panorama from the bow windows of the mansion, taking in woodland plantations, pasture and cornfields and views from the grounds of working windmills and coastal scenes thronged with shipping. Here was a public-spirited as well as a private, domestic landscape, in wartime patriotically useful as well as ornamental, practical as well as pictorial.

Repton's designs also paid close attention to the condition of the local community, the farming and fishing village, for his clients were keen to improve the lot of the local poor. The designs allowed locals to gather wood for fuel, encouraged communal recreation, gave cottages their own gardens and decorated them with shrubs and creepers, created a village green with a maypole in front of the workhouse, and organised communal sports like cricket matches and hare coursing on the beach. If there was a strong element of social supervision to this programme, an attempt to cultivate loyalty in a community vulnerable to invasion by Napoleon's troops, it also reflected Repton's philosophy of landscape gardening. Situating relatively small estates in a wider world, he made private property accessible to a wider public realm of responsibility. At Sheringham, a seaside resort, this extended to allowing tourists into the grounds, at specified times and places, to admire the views.

Repton was never confident that his plans would survive on the ground, given the natural and social changes constantly at work in relation to landscape, but at Sheringham, remarkably, they do. This is in large measure because the property remained in the hands of the Upcher family, who managed changes in the use and working of the landscape with respect to the original design. This included lining Repton's drive with a dramatic display of rare rhododendrons as well as finally, in 1975, building the temple he proposed. Sheringham Park continues to open up to a wider world, and features a series of ecologies, including heathland, grassland and coast.

Houses of Industry

Repton's final published work, *Fragments on the Theory and Practice of Landscape Gardening* (1816), was written at a time when he worried both for the breakup of his profession and the breakdown of British society, the ruin of his life and the landscape at large. In it he holds up the designs for Sheringham as a model of possibility in a world gone wrong. They take their place with two other designs that proved to be significant as models for homes and gardens in the years following. Like most of Repton's designs, they are not completely original but shaped developments that were already underway.

At Sheringham, Repton had proposed making the workhouse less 'an object of terror to the poor, and of disgust to the rich' by making it 'look more like a hospital or an asylum, and less like a prison'. Soon after this commission, he was asked to produce plans for a new 'house of industry', to replace an old poorhouse, a 'wretched building unhealthily placed in wet marshland'. The client was his son Edward, a curate at Crayford, Kent, and the new workhouse was to be built on a newly enclosed heathland, a 'wholesome spot' on the edge of a former gravel pit, and a conspicuous one next to the high road from London to Dover. While the dark north backyard of the building was planned for punishing the able-bodied who refused to work or who broke the rules, a cheerful south-facing terrace was designed as a place of comfort for the old and infirm, with gardens to teach children the tasks of horticulture, to equip them for a world of work, and to sell produce by the side of the road to passers-by.

Repton published the design precisely because it was not carried out, intending it as a public reproach to the parishioners. So delighted were they by what he had made of this unpromising situation, that they decided it should be developed for a greater profit as private houses, leaving the poor to suffer in their present situation.

No matter how well designed and built, workhouses are dark places in the collective memory. Now owned and restored by the National Trust is a workhouse that opened outside Southwell, Nottinghamshire in 1824. It was considered a success because it proved an attractive financial investment to wealthy local property owners. While it may

Left | The imposing front entrance to the workhouse at Southwell, Nottinghamshire. The austere building is the most complete Victorian workhouse still in existence.

Above | Looking down through an open window of the workhouse on to the stark courtyard below. The workhouse was based on prison design.

have been a material improvement on the existing one, the workhouse was designed by its architect to be more like a prison and less like a hospital. Its planner was a local clergymen, the Rev J. T. Becher, who had made his reputation by planning Millbank Penitentiary in London. He declared that the new workhouse was designed not to keep the poor in but to keep them out, by making the place unattractive, a degrading place of last resort. And as such it commanded national attention. Its land and buildings cost more than £6,000 (more than £400,000 in today's money), and the workhouse offered a factory-like economy of scale for the 48 parishes involved, by reducing the costs of poor relief, subsidising wages or giving relief to families themselves. It substantially lowered the rates levied on the wealthy property owners of this cathedral town and surrounding area, while also supplying labour at times of shortage – for harvests, say, or country-house entertainments. The workhouse also made a show of the productive work its inmates performed, for the industrious habits it was presumed to instil as well as the money it saved and made.

Built a mile out of the town, standing impressively on 4 hectares (10 acres) of rising land next to the main road, the workhouse was well built and classically proportioned, with sloping grounds and gardens in front. From afar, it looked like a gentleman's house, one of those severe aristocratic mansions designed to overawe the neighbourhood, before closer inspection made the institutional, disciplinary architecture of this particular powerhouse apparent. Men, women and children were segregated in the workhouse, kept out of sight of each other, families being broken up to do so. If inmates were offered spiritual consolation in the views from the dormitory windows, the spires of Southwell Minster, they were also to be reminded of the clergyman who designed their home and garden. The new moral order of Anglicanism focused on the sins of idleness – of the poor, rather more than the rich.

The vegetable gardens in the front were worked by men when they were not breaking stones in the back yard. The cows grazing the pasture were milked by women when they were not cooking in the basement, working in the laundry, making and mending in the workrooms. Offering a basic diet of milk and potatoes, the workhouse was largely self-sufficient in food. Indeed, it was able to sell surpluses, especially of some of the tastier produce (the soft fruits and leaf vegetables grown within the trim box plots) which does not appear on the inmates' diet sheets. As the regime of the institution changed, so did the grounds. It became a residential home for the elderly in the 1950s and emergency housing for homeless families in the 1970s, the grounds initially maintained by the local council as ornamental gardens of flowers and trees, and now, once again, planted with fruits and vegetables for visitors to buy.

Global Influences on the English Landscape Garden

Many regard the landscape garden as one of the great cultural achievements of these islands, which we have been able to export to other parts of the world. Yet the English landscape garden is itself an amalgam of influences from across the globe, whether the styles of classical antiquity or the latest European fashions and designs. The nineteenth century in particular saw a craze for filling gardens with exotic specimens from far-flung parts, hence the appearance of Chinese or Japanese gardens. Viewed in this light, the plant collectors were evangelists for the modern world of international trade, and gardens an expression of globalisation.

Left | James Bateman created the gardens at Biddulph Grange for his collection of plants from around the world. Different compartments reflect different influences, from Egypt to Italy. The China garden contains the oldest surviving golden larch in Britain, brought from China in the 1850s.

Right | At Stowe in Buckinghamshire, Greek mythology directly inspired the layout of the extensive landscaped garden. The Temple of Concord and Victory is situated on the path of Liberty, and was created to celebrate Britain's victory in the Seven Years' War.

Left | The opening up of Japan to engagement with the West in the second half of the nineteenth century prompted huge interest in Japanese design. The Japanese Garden at Tatton Park, Cheshire, was inspired by a visit to the Japan-British Exhibition of 1910, which drew over eight million visitors in total. The Shinto Shrine and other artefacts within the garden are said to have been imported directly from Japan.

Left | Bodnant Garden in Conwy, Wales, was created in the late-nineteenth century to show off plants from all over the world. The Italianate Terraces were created in the early twentieth century, and the garden has continued to be added to ever since. The Pin Mill building on the Canal Terrace was originally built in 1730 in Gloucestershire, and relocated to Bodnant in 1938.

Below | Inspired by the Mediterranean, cordylines stand in pots around the sundial in Mrs Winthrop's Garden at Hidcote, Gloucestershire. Hidcote is a noted twentieth-century creation, the work of American horticulturist, Major Lawrence Johnston. Like Sissinghurst, it comprises various outdoor 'rooms' featuring a variety of plants and flowers.

Above | The Italian Garden at Mount Stewart, County Down, featuring purple dahlias ('Hillcrest Royal') and palms (*Cordyline australis*) lining the central avenue. The gardens here reflect a rich tapestry of design and great planting artistry that was the hallmark of Edith, Lady Londonderry. The mild climate of Strangford Lough allows the formal areas to exude a strong Mediterranean feel, such that they resemble an Italian villa landscape.

Right | Research has uncovered evidence that South African plants were grown and trialled at Nymans in West Sussex as part of the general collection. As a result, an area historically known as The Wild Garden has been renovated to create the South African Bed. Herbaceous perennials, bulbs, daisies and annuals provide colour and texture to the overall scheme. The resilience of the plants to the English climate is being kept under review.

Suburban Skies

The last design in Repton's *Fragments on the Theory of Practice of Landscape Gardening* was for his own home and garden – not one of the grand houses and parks he designed for others, but a modest villa and garden at Hare Street near Romford in Essex, next to a busy highway. Repton called it his 'humble cottage' and it proved to be the template for middle-class suburban homes with gardens of lawns, flowering shrubs and evergreens, and trellises of climbing roses. Small extensions and strategic planting hid the worst of the surrounding street and secured nicer views, creating a private, domestic realm at the edge of a town, in but not entirely of the local community, semi-detached from the wider world. Here is a strangely familiar domestic setting, a suburban landscape. The National Trust owns some contrasting examples.

'Endcliffe' is a well-to-do tradesman's house built in 1905, on a new road, Blythe Grove, on the edge of the north Nottinghamshire town of Worksop. It has remained largely unaltered since the 1930s: William Straw, the town's leading grocer and seed merchant, died suddenly while gardening in 1932, and his wife followed seven years later. Mr Straw's hat and coat still hang in the hall; the marital bedroom remains untouched other than the old newspapers put on the bed to keep dust off the covers.

The Straws' sons, William and Walter, kept house by keeping things much as they were, without a radio or telephone, let alone television and central heating. William died in 1990, leaving the contents of the house, from old tins of soup to a walnut cabinet, to the National Trust. He had lived so thriftily from the income of the family business and dividends from old Marks & Spencer shares that he also left an endowment of more than £1 million. The Trust purchased the house and the other part of the double villa next door, and restored this mausoleum of family memory as a time capsule of early twentieth-century suburban life.

Its own residents were able to define this home and garden as a heritage site in their own time. To maintain it in its 1930s condition, William, the dominant older son, set out the rules of the house. After a spell in London studying English at Kings College and teaching, he returned to keep the house as it was, even baking bread to his mother's

Left | Mr Straw's House in Worksop, Nottinghamshire. 'Endcliffe', the semi-detached house on the right in this picture, was preserved as a 1920s time capsule by Mr Straw's sons, William and Walter.

recipe with her utensils. He also collected books and researched local history and archaeology. Perhaps unguardedly he donned Levi blue jeans in a 1970 photograph of a local excavation, although such fashion-ware came late to Worksop and a man of his age would have bought them for their original purpose, workwear. While it was not unusual for unmarried daughters or sons to keep the houses as their mother and father left them, living in the past accidentally, it would have required deliberate effort to keep Edgecliffe as it was and the modern world at bay. William seems to have stage-managed its preservation as an antiquarian landmark, including labelling various items for future conservation and museum display.

The two brothers would go about Worksop on a strict routine on Sundays until the 1970s, first to church, and then about the town to check on their shop and allotment, and to see that the footpaths were in good order. In later photographs they look strikingly old-fashioned, diminutive (at a little over 5 feet), bowler-hatted, formally suited, like characters from a silent film or Worksop's answer to performance artists Gilbert and

Above | Two pairs of men's polished black shoes stuffed with paper, displayed in Walter's room.

George. The younger Walter, the town grocer, was actually and unsurprisingly a much more worldly figure, owning a car which his brother made him keep at the shop, and calling into a neighbour's house to listen to the Six O'Clock News before he returned to the 1930s at home.

The wider story, Walter's story, is evident when we consider the gardens as well as the house. In the front garden is an old, but still fruiting, mulberry tree, transplanted by the sons when the family moved from the shop in the centre of town in 1923. William and Walter were grown sons, First World War veterans in their twenties, and Edgecliffe was from the beginning of its arrested development an adult house, with no trace of childhood or growing up. The imprint of the worldlier Walter is evident in the back garden and its now reconstructed greenhouse. A graduate of the RHS cottage and allotment garden course, he raised succulents, importing hundreds of cacti plants and seeds from a German dealer in Mexico, a batch even arriving in 1940 after the outbreak of war.

Over the road (now the visitor car park) was an extensive allotment. Here, and on another show allotment, on the other side of town, Walter cultivated fruit, flowers and vegetables – including luxury items such as asparagus – and raised bees, which supplied produce and seeds for his shop in town. This was when Worksop was booming as the market town in the centre of a modern mining region, albeit one that does not conform to southern stereotypes of such places. It is set in rolling green acres of aristocratic landscape of great estates, with Clumber Park close by. William even collected the novels of the modern laureate of this mining region, D. H. Lawrence. So when we consider the

Above left | The kitchen of Mr Straw's House. The whole house reveals how a grocer's family lived in a Midlands market town between the wars through their furnishings and household items.

Above right | The hallway, with the mens' coats and different types of hats hanging next to the front door.

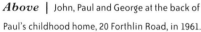

Above | John, Paul and George at the back of Paul's childhood home, 20 Forthlin Road, in 1961.

Above right | John Lennon as a child outside Mendips, the house he lived in with his Aunt Mimi and Uncle George.

entire ensemble of the family home, Edgecliffe was, for much of its life, not a marginal place, not a house that time forgot on the edge of a provincial town; rather it was a family business and gardens, a hub of a flourishing economic and cultural landscape.

By contrast, the homes and gardens that have now been restored in suburban south Liverpool exemplify the cultural importance attached now to ordinary landscapes. The homes where the Beatles John Lennon and Paul McCartney were brought up, now commemorate their formative role in the lives and work of the most influential popular musical partnership in twentieth-century Britain.

The Lennon and McCartney houses were built as part of contrasting developments along two wide arterial roads, Menlove and Mather Avenues, fanning out from the Penny Lane roundabout, 5 miles from the centre of Liverpool. Lennon's house, 251 Menlove Avenue, was the posher development, owned by its residents and identified not just by a number but also by a name – Mendips – taken from the range of Severnside Hills. (This followed a fashion for names taken from the English outdoors.) The house was located on the edge of the old village of Woolton. Following the break-up of his parents' marriage, John lived here with his Aunt Mimi and Uncle George, between 1945 and 1963, from the age of five to 23, along with the student lodgers who helped to supplement the mortgage payments otherwise funded by his uncle's small dairy.

Built in 1933, Mendips has been landscaped to look as it was in 1957, the year Lennon first met McCartney. The restoration is based on a variety of sources, notably family and neighbours' memories and photographs, one of which shows schoolboy John posing politely in his school uniform beside his uncle and aunt. A garage and conifers were removed, neighbouring gardens screened, and a more open-looking garden, appropriate to the time, created. The back garden was devoted to flowers and fruit. Some flowers like lilacs were cut by Aunt Mimi for impressive vase displays in the front room, roses trailed up a trellis outside the east-facing 'morning room', and pink geraniums bordered the lawn that the young John Lennon mowed for pocket money – 'quickly and not well'. Like many post-war suburban households, the garden at

Below | Mendips, the unassuming 1930s semi at 251 Menlove Avenue, Woolton, Merseyside, is now a listed building.

Above left and right | John Lennon's bedroom, and the front porch to which Aunt Mimi would banish the young John and Paul to practise their music.

Mendips was also cultivated for the kitchen, not vegetables but soft fruit, with bushes of gooseberries, blackcurrants and redcurrants.

An only child, Lennon had his own bedroom in Mendips – now valorised by his widow Yoko Ono, a prime mover of the restoration, as the very model of dreamy teenage creativity. Here John and Paul would sometimes work on songs beneath posters of Elvis Presley and Brigitte Bardot, but the room was too small for both left- and right-handed guitarists, and the sound too annoying for the forbidding Aunt Mimi. She banished them to the stained-glass panelled porch looking out on to the front garden, which in any case had a much better, resonant acoustic. Mendips was a bookish household, and this is reflected in the literate lyrics of Lennon's songs, filtered through a range of children's fiction, from Just William to Alice in Wonderland, as well as his aunt's Book of the Month art volumes.

Most of the early music-making was done in McCartney's house, a ten-minute walk away, across a golf course that divided Woolton from Allerton, by Mather Avenue. This was a terrace house on a local authority estate, 20 Forthlin Road. One of a number of corporation estates built after the war to replace old city-centre tenements, many of which had suffered extensive bomb damage, the estate was one of the nicest and a dream house for McCartney's mother Mary. To afford the higher rents, she did two jobs, working as a midwife for the hospital and at the Liverpool cotton exchange. Well planned and architect designed, it had highly specified materials, like ebony doorknobs and brass fittings, as well as a desirable indoor bathroom and toilet. It was, Paul recalls, 'a pleasure to live in'.

20 Forthlin Road had a back garden large enough for his father Jim McCartney, an enthusiastic member of a local horticultural society, who grew dahlias and snapdragons and pot pourri to mask the smell of cigarette smoke in the house. 20 Forthlin Road was empty during the day, and Paul and John, 'sagging off' from school and college, used the living room in the afternoon. The McCartneys' was a hospitable musical household, more permissive than Mendips. The living room had a piano (bought from Brian Epstein's music shop long before he became the Beatles' manager). Paul's younger brother Mike used the kitchen to develop the photos that have been used in the restoration of the house to its later 1950s ambience. Father Jim McCartney was a musician, a former bandleader steeped in music hall, and the house included not only a piano but a radio tuned to popular music, including the only station devoted to

Below left and right | Paul McCartney's family moved into the terraced house at 20 Forthlin Road, Allerton, Liverpool in 1955. It, too, is now a listed building.

Above | The McCartneys' was a music-friendly household and Paul and John would often get together in the living room to work on their song-writing.

pop music, Radio Luxembourg. The radio was rigged up with extension cables and speakers to reach the boys' bedrooms, and they had headphones so they could listen under the blankets.

The Lennon and McCartney homes and gardens were part of a suburban landscape that varied both socially and historically, with plenty of green space and historic associations. It was layered with three centuries of development, first Georgian and Victorian villas, then interwar and post-war private and public housing. Lennon sang in the choir of Woolton village church, where a gravestone announces that an Eleanor Rigby is buried, and which held the summer fête where Lennon's first group, the Quarrymen, made its debut. The municipal golf course, which Lennon and McCartney crossed to each other's houses, was built on a former merchant's landscape park. A few yards from Mendips, was the place recalled in a famous song, the Strawberry Field Salvation Army children's home. This was one of a series of former Victorian villas converted to institutional use, for schools, convents, head offices, hospitals and orphanages. Here the young Lennon attended the annual fête with his aunt, and during the rest of the year he climbed over the wall with his friends to play in the grounds. As well as their own homes and gardens, this wider pastoral landscape exerted a powerful inspiration on the two Beatles, recollected in their music and lyrics – 'there beneath the blue suburban skies'.

Right | A corner of the kitchen at Forthlin Road. Paul's brother, Mike, developed his photographs here, which have been used as reference in the restoration of the house to a 1950s style.

155

Homely Visions

Many National Trust properties are essentially domestic in character. The Country Houses Scheme, after all, was put in place in the 1930s to prevent the demolition of Britain's stately homes – caused, in part, by high tax burdens. Since then, the National Trust has extended its interests by acquiring other kinds of houses. Sometimes this has meant collecting examples of working-class housing before they are lost to the bulldozer and wrecking ball. But equally the Trust has sought to collect houses that are expressions of different ways of living, from Arts & Craft houses to Modernist interiors.

Above | Rosedene, in Worcestershire, is a rare survivor of a Chartist cottage, built for the National Land Company. Founded as the Chartist Cooperative Land Company in 1845 by the Chartist leader Feargus Edward O'Connor, its objective was to give working people a modicum of land, so that they qualified for the vote as well as having a means of supporting themselves through cultivation.

Right | A bedroom at Stoneywell, Leicestershire. Stoneywell was conceived by Arts and Crafts architect-designer Ernest Gimson as a summer home for his brother Sidney. Constructed in 1899, it remained in the Gimson family until 2012 when it passed to the National Trust as an example of the Arts and Crafts approach to domestic space.

Left | Architect Ernö Goldfinger built a terrace of three modernist houses on Willow Road in Hampstead, London, and chose Number 2 as his family home. The design of the buildings, completed in 1939, were the cause of some local controversy. (Ian Fleming lived nearby, and sought revenge by naming one of the villains in the James Bond films after Goldfinger.) Goldfinger also designed brutalist tower blocks, such as Balfron Tower in Poplar.

Above | Nuffield Place in Oxfordshire was the home of
William Morris, Lord Nuffield, motor manufacturer and
founder of the Morris Motor Car Co., from 1933 until his death
in 1963. The image shows Lady Nuffield's Wolseley motor car.
Nuffield Place featured innovations such as automatically
opening gates on the drive, which were activated when cars
passed over hydraulic pads.

Left | Sofa, coffee table and Eames chair in the living room
at The Homewood, Surrey. This Modernist country villa was
designed by the architect Patrick Gwynne for his family and
was completed in the early summer of 1938. The furniture in
the picture was also designed by Gwynne.

Left | A large-format camera, with studio lights in the background, on show at 59 Rodney Street, Liverpool, the studio and home of the celebrated photographer Edward Chambré Hardman and his wife Margaret. Hardman gained a reputation for the quality of his portraits, while he pursued his personal passion for landscape photography.

Above | The boathouse at Greenway, on the River Dart in Devon, the holiday home of the crime writer Agatha Christie. The boathouse was immortalised in fiction as the place where Marlene Tucker was strangled in *Dead Man's Folly*. Christie would spend holidays here with friends and family, relaxing by the river, playing croquet and clock golf, and reading her latest mystery to her guests.

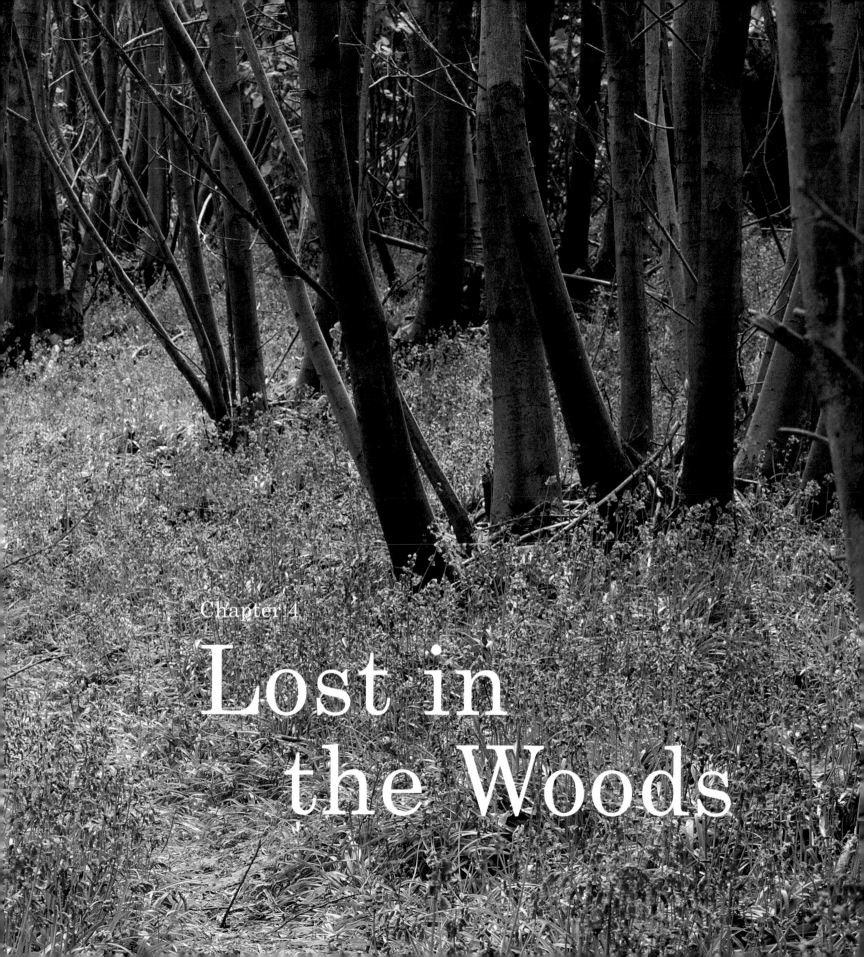

Chapter 4

Lost in
the Woods

Trees, woods and forests are among the most valued features in the landscape, and people respond to them with an emotional intensity that surpasses any other aspect of the natural world. This reflects the many and varied roles that trees and woodlands have played in human culture and society. As with the wider landscape in which they stand, trees hold both material and cultural significance. In past epochs woodlands have sustained entire economies, and they continue to exert a huge influence on the way we think about the world and our place in it. Trees and woods haunt the collective imagination, which is why they are prone, from time to time, to becoming the subject of public and political debate.

The UK has 2.8 million hectares (6.9 million acres) of woodland, which is less than 12 per cent of its overall area. This makes it among the least-wooded countries in Europe, although these figures do not reflect the cover provided by trees in parks, gardens and hedgerows. By the same token, however, the extent of woodland in this country is now considerably more than it was two or three hundred years ago.

Our treatment of trees has regularly become a proxy for wider issues, whether in relation to the government's respect for localities and liberties, the nation's ability to defend itself, or the prevailing level of access to open countryside. The irony is that our landscape has experienced a significant increase in its tree cover at the same time as witnessing a progressive decline in the active agricultural management of those woodlands. Consideration of the competing claims to woodland and its resources demonstrates that forests have periodically become part of a political battleground – one that extends well beyond their own boundaries.

Right | Red deer under the shelter of woodland at Fountains Abbey, North Yorkshire.

Enchanted Woods and Forests

Woods and forests are often regarded as magical landscapes, full of enchantment and wonder. They feature frequently in fairy tales and children's stories, as the places where things are never quite what they seem and where miraculous transformations occur. The enduring appeal of woodlands means that they remain popular destinations for walks and days out. In looking after these places, the National Trust often uses traditional woodland management techniques such as pollarding. This helps to keep alive some of the craft skills and intangible heritage associated with woods and their care, and thereby helps preserve the magic of the forest.

Above | The woods on the Ashridge Estate, Hertfordshire form part of an extensive Site of Special Scientific Interest, comprising a mosaic of habitats from ancient semi-natural and secondary woodland, to bracken and grasslands. Many different types of birdlife are found here as a consequence, including species found rarely elsewhere in Hertfordshire such as redstart, nightingale and wood warbler.

Above | A steep, sandy woodland path through the woods at Wenlock Edge in Shropshire. 'Edges' are the name given to high ground and escarpments. On this red sandstone hill top, copper was mined, and evidence of settlement back to the Bronze Age has been identified here.

Right | The herb garden at Acorn Bank in Cumbria has the north of England's largest collection of culinary and medicinal plants. Nearby orchards contain rare and regional fruit trees. The property gets its name from a bank of ancient oak woodland leading to the waters of the Crowdundle Beck. A giant sequoia was planted here soon after the tree's first introduction from across the Atlantic.

Left | Path and trees at Padley Gorge on the Longshaw Estate in Derbyshire. The estate has been in the ownership of the National Trust since 1931 after being purchased by the people of Sheffield in 1928.

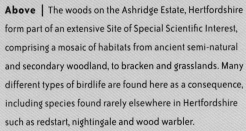

Above | Deer at Dinefwr Park, Llandeilo, Carmarthenshire. The Dinefwr Estate comprises an eighteenth-century landscape park encompassing a medieval deer park and Castle. It has an even longer history of power and influence in the landscape, with evidence for two Roman forts. Wynford Vaughan-Thomas once wrote, 'If you take a handful of the soil of Dinefwr and squeeze it in your hand, the juice that will flow from your hands is the essence of Wales.'

Left | The coppice near Eight Wantz Ways at Hatfield Forest, Essex. Hatfield Forest is a unique survivor of a medieval hunting forest. Oliver Rackham observed that here 'one can step back into the Middle Ages to see what a Forest looked like in use'.

Below | Traditional stone bridge above Aira Force, Cumbria. Aira Force is a 65-foot waterfall, surrounded by ancient woodlands, on the western side of Ullswater. Wordsworth was a regular visitor here, and once wrote of the area that it provided 'the happiest combination of beauty and grandeur, which any of the Lakes affords'.

Above | Lydford Gorge in Devon is the deepest gorge in the South West. Here the fast-flowing River Lyd is bordered by ancient woodland, providing a backdrop to the dramatic sight of waterfalls such as the White Lady Falls. The area is known for its wildlife, including birds such as herons, dippers, wagtails and kingfishers.

Tales of the Forest

The place of woodland in our imagination owes much to its fundamental role in the development of human civilisation. The clearance of trees for farming, commerce and industrialisation has often been seen as a measure of human progress and social cultivation, since landscapes will naturally tend to revert to woodland without human influence. Trees provided raw materials for the new landscapes they made way for, providing timber for building, fuel for heating and charcoal for smelting. In this way, the dark old world of the forest gave way to a bright new world of fields and farms. It is surely no coincidence that in those fairy stories where children stray from their homes and get lost in the woods, they are often saved by the figure of the honest woodcutter – the figure through whom the shady world of pagan superstition is vanquished for a landscape of cultivation, sweetness and light.

Left | Ponies drinking at Dockens Water in the New Forest, Hampshire. The ponies roam freely within the forest, but are owned by New Forest Commoners who hold the rights to the land.

Below | *Jacques and the Wounded Stag: 'As You Like It', Act II, Scene 1*, 1790, by William Hodges (landscape), George Romney (figures) and possibly Sawrey Gilpin (stag) depicts Shakespeare's Forest of Arden. Oil on canvas, Yale Center for British Art, Paul Mellon Fund.

Left | Horse riders at Takeley Hill in Hatfield Forest. As the best surviving example of a Royal Hunting Forest in Britain, it offers us a glimpse of what a medieval English countryside would have looked like.

At the same time, periods of woodland clearance have given rise to anxieties of decline, crises prompted by fears of shortages of the very materials needed to sustain progress or by the ending of traditional woodland ways of life. Though England has become one of the least wooded nations in Europe, its trees and forests assumed a high cultural and symbolic importance from the sixteenth century onwards. Ancient woodland in English literature is mythical and magical, and seldom a dark, forbidding place. Like Shakespeare's Forest of Arden and the Sherwood Forest of the Robin Hood stories, it is not the dangerous and densely disorientating coniferous wilderness of north European legend but a dappled, deciduous Greenwood, a golden world of shady groves and sunny glades. It is, moreover, a place of exile or escape from a world of social oppression, a refuge for lovers and outlaws, dispossessed aristocrats and poor travellers, a place where older freedoms and hospitality may be sustained: Merrie England, in other words.

Within their romantic glades, these literary forests reveal a down-to-earth, social world of herdsmen and huntsmen, woodsmen and wayfarers, of people using the landscape for a variety of livelihoods, including tanning, cobbling, carpentry, foraging and harvesting – of food, medical remedies or fuel. Forests also have industrial uses, such as the production of charcoal for smelting in the Weald, or coal mining in the Forest of Dean, or the burning of bracken for making potash and soap in Needwood and Sherwood Forests.

In reality forests were varied, complex, often open landscapes, not just topographically but also legally. They featured pastures, fields and settlements and implied a range of formal and informal rights and practices. They accommodated a variety of people and claims, from landowners and commoners to customary squatters and vagrants – not always living and working as harmoniously as some poems and stories imagine.

Scholarship on changing woodland communities has revealed their complexity as social landscapes, and the richness of the cultural views they generate. The word 'forest' in England was for centuries an administrative rather than arboreal term, denoting a large territory of many land uses, rather as the term 'national park' does now. In a legal sense, forests were areas of land where the king's hunting rights prevailed. While often wooded, they were not necessarily the woodlands that we imagine today. They were instead areas of wood-pasture, sometimes featuring enclosed farming or grazing lands, but also comprising heaths, moors and mineral workings.

Below | Thomas Gainsborough, *Cornard Wood, near Sudbury, Suffolk*, 1748, oil on canvas, National Gallery, London. As well as a variety of trees and plants, the scene shows a range of incidents, including wood gathering, sand digging, grazing cows and donkeys, sleeping dogs, a couple chatting, and travellers on foot and horseback heading for a distant town.

Forest areas and woodlands have long local traditions of customary and communal management. Common rights of grazing cattle and pigs, of cultivation and the gathering of fuel and wood, were shared among landowners and commoners as well as more informal cottagers and comers and goers. Such rights were intensely local, dependent on custom, tradition and ecology, and confirmed through practice as much as documentation. Common rights in forest areas have myriad local manifestations and inflections.

A complex machinery of governance kept order in the forests, from the forest justiciar to the wardens, foresters and verderers who upheld the forest laws in the courts. The political systems that prevailed in forest areas were not necessarily draconian and adversarial. The propertied in forest areas were granted rights to build mills and make fishponds, dig drainage ditches and even harvest honey from the hives in their trees. Consent to this view of the forest as an open resource was essential to its survival.

Below | The Frithsden beeches on the Ashridge Estate in the Chiltern Hills. Generally, beeches live to 100-150 years, but due to historic pollarding some of the beeches on the estate are 600 years old.

Many forests became more wooded as the hunting rights of the Crown and the grazing rights of commoners were superseded by local landowners planting stands of timber. This was part of a concerted campaign to increase woodland for commercial, recreational and aesthetic reasons. Initially this was done privately, on estates, and then more openly, either by making such places accessible or by planting on publicly owned land. This new arboreal landscape included the hedgerows and plantations of the improved farming countryside and, from the nineteenth century, the private and public parks and gardens of expanding towns and cities. With the collapse of coppicing – the harvesting of trees for poles for a variety of wood products – woods became denser, or converted to timber stands or game coverts. Subtly planted landscape parks became overgrown, their vistas obscured, as trees matured and their protection (by preservation order) increased.

At the same time, sharp differences and disputes arose in the cultural valuation of trees. Surviving ancient trees, centuries old, rose in cultural esteem as they were viewed as the silent witnesses of historical change, becoming increasingly overgrown with myth and legend. While writers cemented the association of Robin Hood and Sherwood Forest for an increasingly urban, industrial readership, so the taste for old, ragged oaks in what remained of the woodland hardened as if for ancient monuments, for ruins of medieval masonry. This high regard for ancient trees and groves was often in contrast to a more caustic view of precocious new plantations, as coppiced deciduous trees vied with stands of coniferous timber for national affection, and 'native' species with exotic ones transplanted from overseas.

Narratives of tree depletion, and the destruction of the landscape as we know and like it, continue to be powerful. Consider the virulent strain of elm disease which took hold in the 1960s or the ash dieback which became a news story in 2012 – both are

cases popularly seen as foreign invasions, from Holland and Denmark respectively. The flattening of whole swathes of trees in southern England in the Great Gale of 1987 is only just starting to be revalued for its ecological and aesthetic virtues, as a stimulus to natural regeneration and the means for clearing away vegetation that had obscured the landscape. The threatened 'sell off' of publicly owned woodlands in 2011, when a new role was envisaged for the Forestry Commission as part of a wider programme of cutbacks, was seen by many as a form of cultural loss, the stripping of a national asset or the termination of public rights of access.

Left | The dramatic split trunk of an ancient hornbeam tree in Hatfield Forest.

Below | Aerial photograph of felled trees on the Petworth Estate, which was taken immediately after the Great Storm of 1987.

Ancient Trees and Liberties

Left | One of the venerable Borrowdale Yews in the Lake District. The three remaining fraternal yews (there were originally four, as noted by Wordsworth in *The Fraternal Four*) are at least 1,500 years old.

The National Trust is the largest of the non-governmental owners of woodlands, with 25,000 hectares (62,000 acres) of woodlands in its care. National Trust woods are a mixture of native woodlands (including ancient woods) and plantations of introduced species, and around 9,000 hectares (22,000 acres) of them are declared as Sites of Special Scientific Interest. Where possible, the Trust maximises the benefits of its trees by managing them actively. They provide places for people to visit, and an estimated 20 million visits a year are made to the Trust's woods. They also supply products of value: round timbers, fencing and construction materials and wood fuel. The Trust removed around 28,000 cubic metres (989,000 cubic feet) of wood from its woodlands in 2011, a quarter or so of the wood grown that year.

Many stands of surviving ancient woodland are found on National Trust land, including some notable legendary trees. These include a famous avenue of pollarded sweet chestnuts at Croft Castle, said to have been planted from nuts from the wrecks of the Spanish Armada; the apple tree that supposedly inspired Isaac Newton's theory

Below | The avenue of sweet chestnuts at Croft Castle, Herefordshire stretches for half a mile to the west of the castle.

of gravity at Woolsthorpe Manor in Lincolnshire; the grove of yews in Borrowdale, Cumbria, glorified by Wordsworth as a natural altar as well as the source of the long bows that won victory at Agincourt; and the Tolpuddle Tree in Dorset, where a group of farm labourers met in 1834 to form the first trade union.

The Ankerwycke Yew, by the Thames opposite Runnymede, is esteemed as a shrine and a silent witness to historical events. Some say it is the place where the Magna Carta was agreed and sealed in June 1215; or where, more than three hundred years later, Henry VIII first met Anne Boleyn. It has stood here for at least two millennia, a fixed point in a landscape that has been constantly changing over the period, as the nearby Thames has shifted its course around and about it. Its canopy and its 10-metre girth have the distinctive misshapen bulk that only ancient trees create. Slowly it is inching across the floor of the wood, sinking its branches into the soil so that they, in hundreds of years' time, will themselves form new offshoots from its main trunk.

Below | The Ankerwycke Yew is thought to be our most ancient tree at 2,500 years old. It stands near the remains of St Mary's Priory across the Thames from Runnymede meadow.

Above | The hollow inside of the ancient Ankerwycke Yew.

The Ankerwyke Yew is a sacred site for a group of modern pagans, and ribbons, feathers and flowers are often found tied to its branches. Small pieces of paper, with yearnings for personal and social healing, are twisted and poked into cracks and crevices in the trunk. The feet of these visitors now compact the soil at the base of the tree, causing a management problem for the National Trust, and a steady stream of visitors might threaten the viability of the tree itself. The Yew stands in the much younger Priory Wood, named after the ruins of an abandoned twelfth-century monastic foundation that lay close by. This wood consists mainly of sycamore, horse chestnut and grey poplar, with an elder, nettle and ivy underfloor. Deadly nightshade is also to be found here, perhaps because it was once cultivated as a medicinal herb by the inhabitants of the Priory.

Whether it was agreed in the shade of Ankerwyke Yew, or across the river on Runnymede's open meadow, Magna Carta had much to say on the subject of woodlands. So much so, in fact, that that the very name 'Magna Carta' – the Great Charter – exists only in order to distinguish it from another charter, the Carta de Foresta – the Charter of the Forest. This was drawn up in 1217, two years after the original charter had been agreed (and then rapidly nullified). The Charter of the Forest expanded on those chapters of the Magna Carta dealing with forest lands and helped to frame the way forest landscapes were to develop for hundreds of years afterwards.

Above | Langham Pond at Runnymede meadow, Old Windsor in Surrey. It formed as an ox-bow lake cut off from the meandering course of the River Thames.

Magna Carta tells us a great deal about the landscape of medieval England. Its fifth clause speaks of 'houses, parks, preserves, fish-ponds, and mills', all of which were familiar sights to the authors of the text. The document might also be interpreted as an early statement of environmental stewardship. Guardians of underage heirs, for example, are exhorted not to 'take from the land of the heir' more than is reasonably due to them, and to do this 'without destruction and waste'. The killer point as far as forests were concerned came in a clause that asserted that 'All forests that have been afforested in our time shall at once be disafforested'. This was a bold step, and represented a significant climbdown for King John given the extent of afforestation that had occurred in his reign. The charter also called for an inquiry into 'All evil customs' and abuses associated with the forests, with a view to ensuring the abolition of such customs after 40 days.

By guaranteeing basic rights of access to natural resources, the Charter of the Forest was arguably more relevant to everyday life than even the Magna Carta. It asserted the freedoms and liberties enjoyed by those living in royal forest lands – rights of grazing cattle and pigs, the right to make mills and fishponds. It remained on the statute book longer than many of the clauses of Magna Carta, not being finally superseded until 1971. Through Magna Carta, the barons aimed to roll back the extension of the forest lands made in John's time, in order to reduce the subjugation of landowners to the forest law and to promote once again their freedom to hold property under common law. Its clauses therefore disclosed the customary relationship that existed between people and the forests, and by extension the wider landscape. The Charter spoke to the long tradition of associating the woodlands with freedoms – the 'liberties of the greenwood', which gave such power and resonance to the story of Robin Hood and his outlaws from the later medieval period onwards.

Home in the Woods

The image of forest dwelling, of cottages in the woods, is a staple of English cultural history. Some of Gainsborough's woodland cottages look so natural, in form and material, that they seem to grow out of the forest itself. This image has been updated with modern ecological woodland building.

Speckled Wood at Swan Barn Farm in Haslemere, Surrey is a new barn-style dwelling, built from timbers that have been sourced from the local woodlands or from other National Trust estates. Dave Elliot, Head Warden for the Trust's Black Down properties, has seen the Speckled Wood project from start to finish. 'There's an entire landscape story here,' he explains, as he gazes over the cruck-timbered main frame, the hand-crafted spiral staircase and the oak floorboards. Adjoining an existing 1980s building, Speckled Wood is an eco-house built from wood that has been grown using time-honoured techniques of forestry management. Four great round-timbered posts support the main joists, while the roof is formed over a frame of sweet chestnut cruck timbers, taken from the Trust's woodlands.

The building is to a design by Ben Law, guru of timber-framed construction and author of *The Woodland Way*, a permaculture approach to sustainable woodland management. Ben's design uses green timbers, a relative rarity these days but an entirely sensible and traditional means of building. The cruck posts are held together using oak pegs. As the chestnut timbers dry over time, they tighten around the pegs, making the structure as solid and firm as any held together by nails and screws. As he looks around, Dave sees through the individual timbers and into the woodlands that surround the building. Every piece of furniture, each fixture and fitting, joist or board reminds him of their place of origin.

Left | The eco lodge Speckled Wood (on the left), which provides volunteer accommodation, and the adjoining Hunter Basecamp, for people on working holidays, at Swan Barn Farm, Surrey.

Swan Barn Farm is a working estate of woodlands and heaths, secreted away in a magical valley just yards behind the main high street of Haslemere in Surrey. The Trust's landholdings here have formed an effective green belt against the pressure of development in Haslemere, an attractive commuter village a little over an hour from London. And so they should, since Haslemere was the chosen home of Robert Hunter, one of the founders of the National Trust, who moved here in 1883 shortly after taking up a post as the Solicitor to the General Post Office. Haslemere still boasts a very fine Post Office building dating from 1907. Hunter would have been proud to have seen and used it, although his death in 1913, just six months after he stepped down from his role at the GPO, denied him the long and happy retirement he had anticipated, tramping over the commons and woods that surround the town.

Lovers of trees, woodlands and forests have many reasons to thank Hunter. He was the architect of the National Trust Act of 1907, and the first Chairman of the organisation, his steely determination and expert legal and political knowledge laying the foundations for today's Trust. Without Hunter, the Trust would not enjoy its special legal powers

of holding land inalienably, 'for the nation', able to sell it only with the agreement of Parliament. But the Trust came towards the end of Hunter's life and career. He is more usually associated with the battles he fought in the 1860s and 1870s on behalf of the Commons Preservation Society, to protect commons and open spaces from enclosure.

Epping Forest was a particularly trying case, one that ultimately had a successful outcome for Hunter and for those people living in and near the forest, who faced the prospect of its enclosure for development. The Epping case began in 1866, when Tom Willingale's son and two nephews were all sentenced to hard labour. Their crime? Selling firewood gathered from ancient forest land around Hainault, which had been fenced off by its owner, the Reverend John Whitaker Maitland. The Commons Preservation Society took up their case and forced the Government into making a concession, although this amounted to an offer of little more than 240 hectares (600 acres) of land for recreation, which was flatly refused. Tom Willingale's death, and the enclosure of more land in Wanstead, led to more pressure on the Government, which announced a Royal Commission into the subject of Epping's enclosure.

Hunter, in his role as legal adviser to the Commons Preservation Society, discovered that the Corporation of the City of London had property interests in Wanstead, and was therefore in possession of common rights over the forest. He persuaded the City, itching for a chance to demonstrate historic freedoms that dated back to Magna Carta, to take up an action against the enclosures in 1871.

Above | Lingwood Common in Essex. For centuries, commoners grazed animals and cut trees and scrub for fuel in the woodlands of Danbury and Lingwood Commons. Today the area is carefully managed in a similar way by the National Trust.

Right | Fifteen views of Epping Forest', a graphic that appeared in the *Illustrated London News*, May 6th 1884.

By the time the case was heard in 1874, Hunter had collected box after box of evidence of common rights in Epping Forest. Evidence of cattle grazing and of the use of forest courts demonstrated that Epping was indeed a common, and that under the Metropolitan Commons legislation, which the Commons Preservation Society had been so influential in introducing, it should not face enclosure. The judge eventually found in Hunter's favour and awarded costs. The Royal Commission, when it reported a year later, came to similar conclusions.

Various Lords of the Manor of Epping, frustrated in their attempts to enclose and draw value from their estates, started to pass their rights over to the Corporation. By 1878 Epping was vested in the Corporation, who to this day retain responsibility for areas of woodland and open land on the fringe of greater London. Loughton's Lopping Hall, erected as compensation to local people for the loss of their common rights, was constructed in 1879. It records in its name the long history of the association of the local people with the woods on their doorstep.

189

Progressive Planting

Left | Rhododendron and azalea in the
Rhododendron Wood planted around 1900 to
create an attractive vista from Leith Hill Place,
Dorking, Surrey.

Movements for planting trees have tended to be consciously modern in outlook, whether in using the latest scientific expertise on plants and soils, new techniques or new species. In the nineteenth century, scenic and scientific principles of tree planting converged, with the rise of the 'arboretum', in which picturesque principles of variety, intricacy and connection were grounded in taxonomy and botany.

At this time the landscape, both in town and country, was in many ways an arboreal as well as an industrial and commercial one. The Victorians made the towns and cities look more natural and the countryside more cosmopolitan, cemeteries suitably shady and venerable, and gardens brighter and more colourful. Arboretums were developed in a variety of sites, scales and settings, including landed estates, public parks, cemeteries, commercial nurseries, the grounds of learned societies and suburban villas. In making space for the systematic collection, propagation and display of trees, and for research and education, arboretums had connections with other expanding institutions of the time, such as museums, galleries, exhibitions, libraries and laboratories. Arborteums demonstrated the power of the British Empire, and its advanced technologies of glass and steel, by importing a great range of species and displaying them geographically. Moreover Britain successfully exported the arboretum as a model landscape, to its imperial rivals like Germany and the United States as well as to its own dominions.

Arboretums were sites of progressive reform, not just in terms of scientific advances but in the spread of such knowledge to the population at large. They were a key site in what was called 'rational recreation' – an improving, family-friendly form of leisure

Right | Woodland path with pale mauve
azalea at Trelissick Garden in Cornwall. In additional
to informal woodland planting, the garden has
formal lawns, dramatic borders, an arboretum and
an orchard.

designed to keep people from less improving excursions, whether to the racecourse or the pub. They managed to blend sufficient entertainment with instruction, spectacle with nature, to attract crowds of visitors. Just a few acres in size, the first public arboretum on the edge of Derby was a sensational success, bringing in packed train excursions from throughout the Midlands.

Though some Victorian arboretums, like Derby, have been renovated as part of urban regeneration, many have now been abandoned or built over. Nonetheless, in their time they successfully spread tree planting, including exotics, to other forms of horticulture and gardening. So called 'woodland planting', with rhododendrons, proved hugely fashionable, for the flamboyant flowering displays that create a botanical theatre of exotic Asian regions. The carriage drive at Sheringham Park was planted with a range of now towering rhododendrons, bringing the Himalayas to Norfolk. This is a fashion of woodland landscaping that has striking continuity with the original design for the grounds at Sheringham by Humphry Repton in 1812.

Indeed, Repton was the man who introduced the word 'arboretum' into England. Envisaging landscapes scenographically, he also promoted the style for exotic planting in his designs of the time for gardens at Woburn and Ashridge. These places displayed their owners' progressive experimental botanical knowledge and were an integral part of a landscape vision for the estate as a whole, including its ancient trees and broadleaved woodland. At Sheringham today the woodland walks include specimen trees of oak, beech and sweet chestnut, some older than Repton's design, as well as a

Right | View from Jupiter Point through woodland planting down to the Lynher River at Antony in Cornwall.

Below | Looking across Rowe's Flashe Lake on a frosty autumnal morning at Winkworth Arboretum in Godalming, Surrey.

Above | The stunning autumn colours of various acers at Winkworth Arboretum in Surrey.

global range of other trees, including Japanese maple, Himalayan birch, Indian horse chestnut, Chinese dove tree, Oregon fir and African Atlas cedar.

Arboretums continued to be developed through the twentieth century to express new currents in the science and art of planting. The National Trust's Winkworth Arboretum (Surrey), which is open to the public throughout the year, was first developed as a private venture in 1937 by Wilfrid Fox. A brilliant dermatologist, he continued his progressive, enlightened mentality in landscape matters as a consultant and planter. He was a prime mover in modern highway design, promoting planting for new arterial roads and bypasses in ways that enhanced their progressive engineering and architecture. Often this was in the teeth of opposition from powerful rural preservationist groups – including, at times, the National Trust. Citing the beautification of the Midlands by the hedgerows of parliamentary enclosure, of the Weald by ash planting in place of the 'jungle growth' felled for iron smelting, and of the Chilterns by new beech wood planted to provide timber for cheap, mass-produced furniture, Fox urged that the new roadscapes of Britain should be beautified for the travelling public by a range of glamorous trees, including the spectacular Asian trees that wealthy gentlemen planted on their private grounds and drives. This modernist, streamlined driving experience was part of a broader, forward-looking vision, one nonetheless obscured by the illusions of timeless tradition. As he declared in 1944, 'the truth is that the scenery of England has changed throughout the ages, and is never static'.

Before its transfer to the National Trust and Royal Horticultural Society in 1952, Fox used his arboretum as a model for reforming the taste in trees. Fox deployed his scientific knowledge of plant and soil chemistry for aesthetic reasons, clearing a 'tangle of hazels and brambles' to reveal some fine ancient beech and mixing in plantings of Korean cherries, Japanese maples, American scarlet oaks and azaleas. This was designed to create a spectacular show of autumn colour (even if some of the Japanese larch had been cut down in 1941 on the orders of the Ministry of Supply for the war effort, for pit props and pulp) and also to remind visitors how exotic trees had always been naturalised into the landscape. In a paper to the Royal Horticultural Society, Fox reported that on one occasion he took an artist friend 'who was of the last ditch, die hard "only English trees to be planted" school', to overlook the valley where he planned the arboretum.

Then he turned to me, asking if I really meant to defile this beautiful valley, this characteristic English landscape with trumpery little splashes of foreign trees and shrubs. Timidly, but I confess with malice aforethought, I asked him to point out the English trees he so admired. He replied: 'Why look at that lovely stretch of mauve-pink planting up the valley followed by a mass of wavey green'. I need hardly tell you that the mauve pink was a belt of Japanese Larches and the green a plantation of Douglas fir, both introduced about the middle of the last century.

Below | Mist rises from the lake as the morning sun catches the tops of the trees behind the boathouse at Winkworth Arboretum.

Non-Native Trees

The Victorians had a fashion for introducing exotic species of trees into their parks and gardens. Fine specimens, such as sequoia and monkey puzzle trees, are often to be found in National Trust places. These trees can grow to great sizes, and become integral features within a landscape. They speak to the fact that landscapes are invariably mixtures of the native and non-native, a line that is in any case sometimes blurred and difficult to discern. The sweet chestnut, for example, is a ubiquitous feature in the landscape today, yet it is a non-native species that was introduced by the Romans.

Above | Giant sequoia at Sheffield Park. *Sequoiadendron giganteum* was brought to England from California in the middle of the nineteenth century by William Lobb, plant hunter for the Veitch Nurseries. The tree grows to heights of 90 metres or more. It quickly became a popular and high-status adornment to estates in Britain.

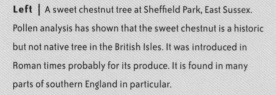

Left | A sweet chestnut tree at Sheffield Park, East Sussex. Pollen analysis has shown that the sweet chestnut is a historic but not native tree in the British Isles. It was introduced in Roman times probably for its produce. It is found in many parts of southern England in particular.

Above | This giant redwood tree (*Sequoiadendron giganteum*) stands in the garden at Killerton in Devon. Killerton's landscape owes much to John Veitch, the horticulturalist and nurseryman, who was employed here by Sir Thomas Acland. Because of Killerton's mild climate, Veitch was able to introduce many exotic species.

Right | A monkey puzzle tree (*Araucaria araucana*) on the terrace at Arlington Court, Devon. The tree was originally found in central and southern Chile and western Argentina, and was introduced to Britain in 1795. It is said that it derives its English name because it was such a puzzle as to how monkeys could climb the branches, although monkeys are not in fact indigenous to the tree's South American home.

Above | The Wellingtonia Avenue at Biddulph Grange garden, Staffordshire. The garden was designed in the mid-nineteenth century by James Bateman to display his extensive plant collection. Wellingtonia is an Anglicised name for the sequoia or giant redwood, in contrast to the name preferred by some on the other side of the Atlantic, the Washingtonia.

Right | A cedar tree was planted by Kaiser Wilhelm II in 1907 when he visited Kingston Lacy in Dorset. A number of other cedar trees on the estate have historic associations, such as the Duke of Wellington cedar. Although this cedar has now been removed due to its age, seedlings have been cultivated to enable a new tree to be planted in the same location.

Above | View through the Lower Stream Garden at Trengwainton in Cornwall, showing the *Dicksonia antarctica*, a species of evergreen ferns native to eastern Australia.

Left | This is a view of the Pinetum at Biddulph Grange, Staffordshire. Pinetums were plantations of coniferous trees, highly popular in the nineteenth century as a means of showing off the range of imported plants that owners had adopted on their estates.

New Forests

Trees are often seen as traditional features, natural and rural, which makes it harder for them to be recognised as belonging to the modern, progressive era, yet new plantations are just as much a feature of the landscape as historic woodlands.

The largest and most widespread campaign of progressive planting was conducted by the Forestry Commission. The state-owned Commission was established in the immediate aftermath of World War I, to oversee the management of the publicly owned forest estate (principally Crown lands) and also, in the face of severe timber shortages, to undertake large-scale uncompromisingly commercial planting for timber production.

Many of the conspicuous large coniferous plantations of the Forestry Commission were located on open mountain and moorland, which had no forest history or at least no continuous one in cultural memory. Such planting was not entirely new, for large aristocratic landowners in such regions had afforested tracts of land with pines and larches, but it encountered criticism in more publicly accessible uplands with existing broadleaved woodland. Wordsworth had been famously critical of large larch plantations for disfiguring the Lake District, not just for their artificial appearance but for symbolising the incoming commercial and industrial interests that disrupted traditional local scenery and society. Such new plantations, he declared in his *Guide to the Lakes*, contrasted with the harmony of a traditional woodland community, preventing 'that fine connexion of parts, that sympathy and organization, if I may so express myself, which pervades the whole of a natural wood'.

The Forestry Commission conducted a publicity and education campaign to promote coniferous landscape beauty, praising its functional modernist design and describing it as clean, bright and efficient. In its Guide Books it even imagined that visitors might make special trips to view examples of good practice in nursery management. Here was an explicitly heroic social vision, of government-directed reconstruction and development, reminiscent of 1930s New Deal America or even Soviet Russia. By locating the historic roots of this new coniferous landscape in continental European tradition, including nations like Germany which had a long tradition of state forestry,

Left | Razed forest of pine trees stripped for timber at the Forestry Commission coniferous plantation in Galloway Forest Park, Argyllshire.

Above | *Entrust*, a wooden sculpture by Rosalind Rawnsley at Brandelhow, Derwentwater in Cumbria. Rosalind is the great-granddaughter of Canon Hardwicke Rawnsley, one of the founders of the National Trust.

the Commission sought to connect the uplands of England with those of Scotland and Wales in a Gothic British vision.

For its plans further south for the New Forest and the Forest of Dean, the Commission professed to be maintaining a modernised and professionalised continuity with the common people, rather than the leisured aristocratic interests which had for centuries oppressed them: 'the woodland warning "Beware of mantraps and spring guns" will still be within the memory of some of us,' pointed out the President of the British Society of Foresters in 1939.

While Forestry Commission plantations increased by 400 hundred per cent, to around 162,000 hectares (400,000) acres by 1938, getting on for half the UK's ancient woodland was cleared or substantially damaged by plantation forestry in the second half of the twentieth century. As the demand for timber became less acute and issues of biodiversity assumed a high cultural and public profile, the Commission conceded ground, and southern English tastes for deciduous trees were accommodated. After nearly a century of activity, the Commission holds around 15 per cent of the country's total woodlands, but has sufficiently modified its radical coniferous origins and hardline commercial cropping imperatives, to command a broader consensus of popular support. Supporting ecological values and promoting picturesque aesthetics, including the installation of environmental artworks along forest sculpture trails, has helped to raise the Commission's cultural profile.

The Far North

The road to Kielder Forest from the south is to the border country between England and Scotland, passing Hadrian's Wall to a cultural frontier in the appreciation of woodland scenery. Far from the dappled greenwood and hedgerows of southern England, we come to a scene that some visitors find reminiscent of Scandinavia or Canada, a great lake reflecting a big sky, surrounded by extensive stands of dense coniferous forest. This is not a primordial scene of nature but a recently created one, the woodland planted by the Forestry Commission from the 1920s and the lake created in the 1980s. This, declares the visitor centre, is the largest forest in England, the largest manmade lake in northern Europe, and it has the darkest night skies in England and the biggest reserve of its red squirrels. Here is England's Great Outdoors.

There was once an ancient forest here, of which the small stands of Scots pine may be surviving relics, as are pockets of peat land. However, a long history of management for grazing, then grouse shooting, kept the vegetation down, and the coniferous woodland is consciously modern. The strategic need for timber in the mid-twentieth century was met by planting rows of fast growing, high yielding Sitka spruce, which thrived in these uplands. The forest is still intensively cropped and harvested but as the need for home-

Below | A fishing boat on Kielder Water, a large artificial lake in the Kielder Forest Park in Northumberland.

grown timber has become less pressing, and the importance of the location as a visitor attraction increased, so spruce monoculture has been broken up by other species and the edges of planting zones contoured to make them seem more natural.

This is a paradoxical place. Planting more 'native' species of broad-leaved trees might naturalise the landscape but it would also create a habitat for an animal seen as invasively 'alien', the grey squirrel, and it is on a coniferous reservation here that the iconic red squirrel survives. Like the osprey, another conservationist icon promoted for visitors in Kielder, red squirrels are seldom glimpsed; Kielder Forest's cornucopia of larch and pine cones brought south flocks of other birds, such as siskins and crossbills. The lake has also attracted other exotic species, including the Mandarin duck once introduced to decorate the water of landscaped parks.

Kielder Water, a reservoir, also belongs to the modernist, twentieth-century age of planning and projection. Its large-scale engineering has roots in both an older north-east culture of landscape – industrial Tyneside – and a technologically advanced country estate like Cragside – the first house in the world to be lit by hydro-electricity. Fears of water depletion in the face of industrial demand prompted large-scale large dam building, the water here being channelled to the industries of Teeside and a power station added to generate electricity. As with other such projects, the regional and national interest was considered to outweigh the impact on the local inhabitants displaced by flooding the valley. The dam was landscaped, given a double curvature to echo natural slopes, and the surroundings designed with sweeping vistas from wide US parkway-style roads, discretely dotted with tourist timber cabins.

Kielder Water and Forest Park are now in the hands of a private consortium, and the wider interest is now seen as recreational rather more than industrial. The area is promoted as an all-season, all-weather attraction, a playground for people from all social groups, for walkers and cyclists as well as drivers and people travelling by bus from Newcastle, some to enjoy the north-east's Winter Wonderland. It is still a projection, a landscape in the making: the promotional 'A Bird's Eye View in 2035' imagines a more bio-diverse wooded lakeside and extends the invitation 'Welcome to a Vision of the Future'.

Like other reforming state organisations founded in the twentieth century, the Forestry Commission commands a degree of public affection, its esteem as a national treasure rising in the face of threats to strip its assets. In early 2011, the newly elected coalition government in Britain published a consultation document on the future of the national public forest estate. In ordinary times there would be nothing especially unusual or provocative about this, given that governments issue consultations on new policy proposals all the time. Yet this particular consultation, coinciding as it did with

Kielder Forest Park, Kielder, Northumberland, 11 April 2014
by Simon Roberts.

a significant programme of cuts in public sector budgets, led to a firestorm of protest and opposition, as local groups rose up to demand that the government perform a rapid reversal of its plans.

What went so wrong? The consultation anticipated that the Forestry Commission might forge itself a new role. It would no longer be the sole owner and manager of a vast forest estate, and large parts of this land would be sold or transferred to other, non-governmental management. Commercial forests would be sold to private business groups, while the less commercial 'heritage' forests (including the Forest of Dean and the New Forest) would be transferred to charities or to community management.

A measure that offered simultaneously to reduce the public sector deficit while promoting local or civic control over forest lands might, in other contexts, have aroused little controversy. And yet the outrage sparked by the consultation was sufficient to lead the government to take the unusual step of pulling the consultation in its entirety halfway through the period designated for comments. The calls of 'Save our Woods' and 'Hands off our Forests' won the day, as the government was cast in the role of the desecrator of the nation's patrimony and heritage, the feller of our mighty national forest estate.

In truth, the public forest estate in the UK amounts to less than a fifth of the total forest lands. The sorts of sales and transfers that were proposed had been happening for years on a smaller scale, and might have been permissible under different economic and political conditions. The environment and landscape rarely feature in newspaper headlines, but this particular consultation seemed to hit a nerve. It was viewed as nothing less than an attack on the soul of the nation.

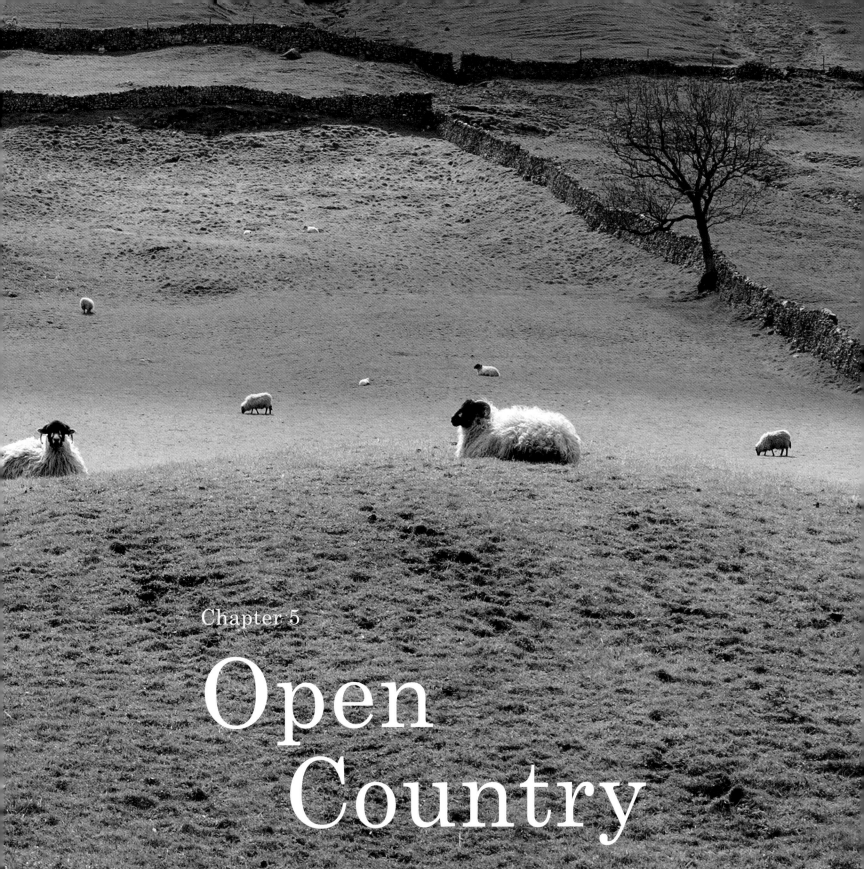

Chapter 5

Open Country

your **BRITAIN** · *fight*

DAMS BROS. & SHARDLOW LTD.

ISSUED BY A·B·C·A

The South Downs

FRANK
NEWBOULD

or it now

DESIGNED BY P.R.2.B

Some of the most powerful images of the countryside are expressly patriotic ones, produced in response to threats to the nation as a whole. The poster 'Your Britain – Fight for it Now', designed by Frank Newbould and produced by the War Office in 1942, shows a rural scene on the South Downs. In the foreground a shepherd and his two dogs herd a flock of sheep along a rolling hillside as they look across to woodland cover. A cluster of farm buildings nestles in the fold of the landscape below them. A tower sits on top of a hill in the middle distance, while on the horizon there is a glimpse of the English Channel, beyond which lay occupied France and the threat of invasion.

This was one image in a series called 'Your Britain – Fight for it Now'. Churchill objected to another in the series, showing the shining new Finsbury Health Centre, behind which was a ruined slum inhabited by a child with rickets. It was later withdrawn. Evidently, people in a now largely urban and industrial nation, many with immediate memories of poverty and disease, were presumed, or expected, to be uplifted by a pastoral scene, one of rolling rural acres.

Churchill had good reason, though, to expect people to respond patriotically to such rural scenes, despite or perhaps because of their urban home. Town and city dwellers of all kinds made excursions to the countryside, whether hiking or motoring. The poster of the Downs was in much the same style as the numerous prints that Newbould had produced before the war for railway and petrol companies, to advertise the delights of the countryside and coast. These depicted places throughout Britain, including Wales and Scotland, but there was a particular focus on English landscape, particularly southern landscapes that were within convenient reach, by road and rail, of London.

The chalk downland near the coast became a favoured form of scenery in the earlier twentieth century. As shown in Frank Newbould's image, it combined an expansive sense of open country with a more enclosed sense of domestic comfort signified by the sheltered farmhouse. The landscape is both prospect and refuge, facing robustly outward as well as securely inward. The poster itself is not conventionally picturesque or

Left | Frank Newbould, 'Your Britain – Fight For It Now', 1942, Imperial War Museums. A patriotic wartime poster showing a rural scene of the South Downs with a shepherd and his dogs herding sheep.

Previous page | Sheep grazing at Wharfedale, Yorkshire. The dales you see today are a managed landscape shaped by human intervention over hundreds of years.

traditional. Indeed it has a striking, streamlined modern style, with a motor road in the distance. It is an image of the whole 'open air movement' of the mid-twentieth century, which was enlisted for the war effort, the modern speeding travellers juxtaposed with the shepherd and his flock in the foreground.

Many illustrated books on the countryside were not only guides to rural places but were guides for untutored townspeople on how to see and appreciate the countryside, the life and work of village people and farming folk as well as the nature and history of landscapes. Harry Batsford's book *How to See the Country*, published in 1940 as part of the Home Front series, served just this purpose. 'It is our heritage, and we are going to share in its breezy, kindly spirit in spite of all adverse factors, be they from an external enemy or internal restrictive machinations … We are going to see the country and live.'

For Batsford, the countryside was a rich tapestry of forms and colours. He recounted an anecdote of meeting a party of three French people on a bus. After failing adequately to explain what the word 'common' meant on their bus tickets, he spent an enjoyable afternoon with them on 'the endless purpling heaths and scrub coppices' above Midhurst. By contrast, he was scathing about a coach party of East Enders who had stopped on Berkhamsted Common: 'They produced a gramophone and started foxtrotting on the turf.' These cockneys had clearly not learned to see the country aright and conduct themselves accordingly. Commons might not, it seems, be for the common people.

While roaming on the commons with an educated eye was one of Batsford's pleasures, he reserved his greatest admiration for the hedgerows that create 'one of the most characteristic features of the English scene'. For Batsford, hedges contributed to 'the trimness which gives a gardenlike appearance to English farmlands' and were a demonstration of the English love for 'neat orderliness' – in life as in landscape. Best seen from a height, hedged fields offered that quilt-like tidiness that is characteristic of English landscape taste of the time, especially as portrayed in the covers of the popular Batsford series of countryside books. But the image was not as timeless as it seemed.

Enclosure

The countryside of much of lowland England was changed beyond recognition by the process of enclosure, gradually from the sixteenth century, then more dramatically in the later eighteenth and early nineteenth centuries. The act of enclosure imposed a new legal framework on to the traditional working landscape. Instead of open fields and commons being managed collectively, regulated by the manorial courts, enclosure parcelled the landscape up among individual owners, to be managed separately and independently. As well as creating a more private landscape of hedged fields, woodland plantations, walled parks and outlying farmsteads, the grid of enclosure realigned communications, stopping up old pathways, ending rights of way, and creating new or straightened roads. Effectively it mobilised the countryside for a modern market economy, making it look more visibly prosperous to the passing traveller. The

Below | Natural hawthorn hedging on the Isle of Wight. Fast-growing hawthorn hedgerows were planted as a result of the eighteenth-century Enclosure Acts.

consequences of enclosure were still being felt a century after it had achieved its greatest extent – and, it could be argued, are still being felt today.

Enclosure put an end to many relationships with the landscape that were more customary and informal, and more dependent on mutual cooperation. In a typical pre-enclosure village, two or three large open fields would be shared among village farmers, each of whom had rights to farm individual strips scattered across them. Land lying outside these fields was designated as 'waste', and here individual farmers might possess different levels of right to graze cattle or use it in other ways. These uses included rights to take off peat or turf for fuel (a right known as common of turbary); to take wood, reeds or other vegetation for general uses (common of estovers); to graze pigs in woodlands or forests (common of pannage); to take fish from lakes or streams (common of piscary); and in some cases to take soil, minerals or wild animals.

These common rights varied from place to place, depending on the nature of the local environment, the types of farming practised, and the form of the landscape itself. In many areas they were assigned to particular plots of land and thereby considered the inheritance and property of individual farmers, who in turn were merely the tenants of the Lord of the Manor.

PARTE OF

PARTE OF ECMONTON

KIRTON

LORDSHIP

LORD

ship

PARTE OF

OMPTON

LORD

ship

PART OF

RVFFORD ABB

FIELDES

LORD

OSSINGTON

PART

OF THE

PARTE

OF THE

PARTE OF

LORDSHIP OF KARSALL

PARTE OF

ESTON LORDS:ᴾ

OSSINGTON

HIP OF

Left | Map of the Manor of Laxton, 1635, The Bodleian Library, University of Oxford. The map shows strips in open fields. Today Laxton remains an 'open field' farming village with the medieval system still in place.

Common land in Britain holds a special place for people concerned with the public value of landscape. Research is revealing it to be highly complicated physical and cultural terrain, much less understood than many of its admirers or detractors might assume. Only at places like Laxton in Nottinghamshire do we today come close to understanding what the medieval landscape might have resembled. Here, three open fields are still managed in common by local residents, an echo of what much of the countryside of midland and southern England would have looked like in the early eighteenth century: unfenced, open and, to promoters of enclosure, unappealing, bleak and confusing, far from picturesque.

Enclosures could be carried out by individual or collective agreement – as, indeed, the vast majority were before 1700. The sixteenth century saw a wave of enclosures by powerful landowners, for the purpose of grazing sheep, to power the woollen trade. Their actions went unhindered, though there were protests at the eviction of people to make way for sheep, the shadow side of a sunny pastoral scene.

Those lands that remained unenclosed, however, often had such a complex variety of legal rights and obligations over them that recourse to Parliamentary Act became a more frequent method for carrying out enclosures. Between 1750 and 1830, the peak of the enclosure movement, around 4,000 individual enclosure acts were passed in this way. The passing of an Act was the starting gun for a process that could last up to eight years or more, during which time groups of commissioners and surveyors, usually outsiders, would descend on a village and agree awards of land holdings to individuals according to the extent of their interest in and over the soil. In place of shared strips in the open field and rights of common over the wastes, individual fields were first parcelled up on paper and then fenced on the ground with the distinctive hawthorn hedgerows that predominate across the countryside today.

The pace and scale of enclosure varied from parish to parish, but in many areas it had a profound impact. The loss of common rights over the open fields – for grazing animals on the stubble left after the harvest, for example – as well as the loss of whole tracts of commons themselves, had consequences for the social and economic life of the countryside. In turn there were manifold cultural ramifications because landscapes that had previously been regarded as communal and customary resources were reframed as wholly private territory. Instead of vast open fields, with their generous headlands and

ridge-and-furrow corrugations, smaller individual fields predominated, often sharply rectilinear – first envisaged by the surveyor's theodolite and projected on to paper and new maps and then made on the ground. Traditional customs were now more tightly regulated, even curtailed, including gleaning, the gathering of the small amounts of grain left by the harvest. That gleaning is a custom also described in the Bible helped fuel moral criticism of the enclosure process.

This sudden change in the form and nature of the landscape might have been stark, but the process was more often than not consensual. The cases of enclosures that were contested are few and far between, not least because grievances were usually addressed in the course of bringing an enclosure bill to Parliament or during the drawn-out process of making the enclosure award. Few farmers denied that farming in severalty was a more efficient approach than seeking to agree decisions through the manor court. Scholars have debated the topic endlessly, but it seems certain that enclosure helped facilitate the sort of agricultural innovations that transformed the productivity of the countryside in the eighteenth and nineteenth centuries: new crops, new ploughing techniques, new fertilisers.

But there were losers too. Those with little interest in the land at the point of enclosure, and few if any rights to graze or share other common resources, might be

especially worse off as the result of the dismantling of medieval forms of communal land management. Others, with only a marginal existence on the fringes of village society, such as labourers with no direct property interests, would certainly have been hit hard by an enclosure. Such classes often depended greatly on a more customary relationship with the land, whereby they took from it animals or crops on the basis not of strict legal right under manorial law, but localised consent. Customary rights were lost at enclosure and no compensation offered. Moreover, the fencing in of the wider landscape would have greatly altered the way that landscape was experienced and perceived on a daily basis. Traditional rights of way across it could be rerouted or possibly ended, landmarks like ancient trees uprooted, so that familiar scenes might be lost, inhabitants disoriented, their sense of place put into doubt.

It is hardly surprising, then, that from time to time the act of enclosure was interpreted as an act of aggression and gave rise to direct resistance. Some anti-enclosure events have been widely publicised, and have become iconic episodes in radical histories of rural England focusing on landscape as a record of dispossession. At Otmoor in Oxfordshire the enclosure of the common provoked a local uprising, as a crowd of up to five hundred turned out in September 1829 to destroy the new fences and hedges that had been erected on the open moor. The cry 'Otmoor for ever!' was frequently repeated as night-time skirmishes against the enclosures continued over the winter,

often conducted by locals in disguise – men with blackened faces, sometimes dressed as women, often carrying weapons. The opponents, a group of whom were dramatically rescued from police custody after they had been taken under armed guard to Oxford, were striking a blow for the disappearance of a whole way of life centred on the common, and for a customary relationship with the landscape that was disappearing forever.

Enclosure changed the face of many midland counties. They became more ordered, planned landscapes, in which farming was a serious business. But despite its striking visual impact on the landscape, parliamentary enclosure can obscure longer-term and more subtle processes and experiences of change and continuity. Even in Northamptonshire, the epicentre of the parliamentary enclosure movement, the rural world was not suddenly and completely transformed, as the work of Briony McDonagh at Hull University and Matthew Cragoe at Sussex University has shown. Field closes, enclosures managed outside the communal arable system but still seasonally thrown open to common grazing, prefigured more formal enclosure arrangements, as they also did in other parts of England. And while privately owned land was not always physically hedged, hedgerows were far from an unknown feature in the pre-enclosure landscape, and nor was that countryside as bleak or unvaried as enclosure's advocates would argue.

Parliamentary enclosure did not always signal a sudden and catastrophic end to traditional and communal ways of life. For example, the architecture and ceremonies of the local church might be little affected, with Church-sponsored customs, like vermin control, the killing of birds and animals that destroyed crops, continuing across the newly privatised fields. Such acts were not recognised as trespass in common law, and villagers used the custom as cover to pursue game (which was illegal). Enclosure in this way neither completely closed down access to the countryside nor brought an end to traditional ways of life.

Farms and Farm Buildings

We are an agricultural nation, and the architecture of our farms and farm buildings is often much cherished and admired. Some redundant barns are now protected as unique examples of their kind due to their antiquity and scale. The era of agricultural improvement and high farming in the eighteenth and nineteenth centuries witnessed significant investment in the physical infrastructure of farms: new buildings (often in brick) enabled ever-more productive agricultural techniques to be deployed. Historic farm buildings in this way speak to centuries of economic progress and development, even as their ongoing care and maintenance can remain a conservation challenge.

Above | The Dovecote at Willington in Bedfordshire stands near an associated set of stables. Both buildings were constructed in the mid-sixteenth century, probably from stone robbed from local priories after the Dissolution of the Monasteries. The buildings were saved from the threat of demolition in the first half of the twentieth century and donated to the National Trust.

Left | The Cider House on the estate at Godolphin House, near Helston, Cornwall. This is the oldest agricultural building on the estate, and was in a parlous state until relatively recently. Thanks to a legacy of a benefactor with close links to the estate, it was possible to employ local craftspeople to use traditional methods to restore the building.

Above | Cauliflower and other vegetables growing in the Kitchen Garden, Clumber Park, Nottinghamshire. Clumber was originally one of the aristocratic Dukeries estates carved out from Sherwood Forest. Although the house at Clumber was lost in the 1930s, it remains a hugely popular draw for visitors. The kitchen garden contains the longest stretch of glasshouse of any cared for by the National Trust.

Right | A combine harvester brings in the crop in the farm fields surrounding Sissinghurst Castle, near Cranbrook, Kent. The National Trust aims to reconnect the garden at Sissinghurst with the surrounding farm landscape, by creating a vegetable garden to supply the restaurant with organic produce and by re-establishing the farmland as a mixed Wealden farm, such as would have existed in 1930 when the property was bought by Vita Sackville-West and Harold Nicolson.

Left | Interior of a timber-framed monastic grange barn built around 1140–50 in Coggeshall, Essex. Now cared for by the National Trust, the barn faced ruination in the 1970s even though it is one of the oldest examples of its kind anywhere in Europe. It was restored thanks to the efforts of local people.

Below | The mid-thirteenth-century monastic Great Coxwell Barn near Faringdon in Oxfordshire. The barn is the sole surviving part of a medieval grange that provided income to Beaulieu Abbey. Built from Cotswold rubble-stone walling, the building is a reminder of the wealth of the great monastic orders. It was a favourite of William Morris, who called it 'unapproachable in its dignity'.

Above | The home farm at Wimpole was to a design by Sir John Soane, architect of the Bank of England among many other buildings. It demonstrates the pursuit of agricultural improvement in the eighteenth-century, featuring barns, cattle sheds and stables ranged around efficient and accessible courtyards. The Wimpole Estate remains a place where agricultural innovation is shared and promoted, since it is one of the few farms to be managed in-hand by the National Trust.

Right | A barn on the Blickling Estate in Norfolk. The National Trust is responsible for a great many buildings in the landscape around Blickling, some of which have been restored in recent years, and are now leased out to tenants or as holiday cottages.

The Old Ways

So powerful has enclosure proved in lowland England, as a generic process, and so settled is our view of the English countryside as a patchwork of fields enclosed by hedges, walls and fences, that it is hard to envisage how landscapes of open fields and commons looked. It is a landscape that must be reimagined from the traces that survive on the ground, and from historical evidence – from art, literature, and documentation of the enclosure process. This includes the evidence of those who opposed it, through direct action such as riot, trespass and hedge-breaking, as well as litigation and parliamentary counter-petitions.

Complaints about enclosure were not just grass-roots popular protests. There is a considerable literature of anti-enclosure sentiment from traditional conservative landed interests who had lost ground in the new modern, commercialised countryside, as well as from middle-class country lovers who found barriers to their presumption to roam rural England for recreation. Indeed the very word enclosure expanded, beyond a legal, material process, to become a metaphor for a more widespread sense of exclusion and dispossession.

The pre-enclosure landscape persists powerfully in the popular imagination, as a cultural memory, if often a mythical one. It is a landscape, like so many in the cultural imagination, that signifies a sense of loss, and like so much rural folk memory is marked by a good deal of wishful thinking, fabrication, even invented tradition. Attachment to the old ways in England has the added provocation of continuing a sense of injustice, as private interests are seen to enclose the public good in other ways. Indeed the loss of commons, real or imagined, has been a major spur in campaigns to preserve public open space and with it a sense of recovering or remaking cultural as well as material common ground.

Much landscape art celebrates an enclosed landscape, a neat garden-like countryside of hedged fields, woodland plantations, parks and pleasure grounds, a landscape of private property, often landed estates, albeit visible for a wider public from roads

Right | John Sell Cotman, *A View of Mousehold Heath from Silver Road*, c.1810, watercolour, British Museum. A significant area of Mousehold Heath outside Norfolk escaped enclosure. Gradually woodland encroached on the open landscape but some parts of the original heath survive today.

and pathways. And during the great age of landscape art during the eighteenth and nineteenth centuries, the purpose of such pictures was not to portray a traditional or timeless idyll but rather to show dramatic, modern improvements to a more open, collectively managed countryside, one that was found more commercially as well as more pictorially appealing than the territory of open fields and heaths.

But if we look closely and widely, art and literature can also offer us a record of the common field landscape. This could be consciously a matter of memory, of nostalgia for a countryside that was past or passing, of a world we have lost, or a commentary on the contrast of common and private land. Such art could also be more affirmative, even campaigning, its imagery harnessed to conserve and enhance those more public, open spaces that remained.

Below | Purple heather decorates the open heathland of Rockford Common in the New Forest, Hampshire.

Many early eighteenth-century landscape paintings and prints, made before the period of dramatic parliamentary enclosure in lowland England, show extensive commonable fields, meadows, forest and heathland around country houses, towns and cities – in part as a matter of record, because it was there. At the same time, these prospects were keen to contrast the neat, intensely developed, enclosed sites of mansions and towns with a more open country, used for the recreation of the wealthy (like hunting and promenading) as well as the livelihood of the poor (like wood and bracken gathering). This was a broad social vision of the countryside, albeit one centring on urban and rural sites of power and privilege.

Some landscape art, mindful of the antiquity of sites and scenes, focuses on the longstanding significance of common landmarks. In the 1720s, a century before parliamentary enclosure transformed the local Northamptonshire countryside, Peter Tillemans recorded a view of an old tree 'Langdyke Bush' on the open tract of Helpston Heath, considering it to be just as much a part of the history of the county as the architectural antiquities he recorded elsewhere. Langdyke Bush was an ancient landmark for the community, the site of an open-air medieval court, but it also had a darker history as the site where a gibbet once stood, and Tillemans depicted it shortly after this was dismantled.

'Langley Bush', as it is also called, is famous now for its literary associations. Well over a century after Tillemans' picture, the poet John Clare lamented the cutting down of the tree as part of the enclosure of the heath. It was not so much a communal landmark as an emotional one, recalled as a place of childhood play in a poem *Remembrances*, which mixes personal grief with political anger.

By Langley Bush I roam, but the bush hath left its hill,
On Cowper Green I stray, tis a desert strange and chill,
And the spreading Lea Close oak, ere decay had penned its will,
To the axe of the spoiler and self-interest fell a prey,
And Crossberry Way and old Round Oak's narrow lane
With its hollow trees like pulpits I shall never see again.
Inclosure like a Buonaparte let not a thing remain,
It levelled every bush and tree and levelled every hill
And hung the moles for traitors – though the brook is running still
It runs a sicker brook, cold and chill.

As enclosure progressed, so painters, like poets, contrasted common land and peasant livelihood with the new world of walled parks and gardens, hedged fields and hard work. They sometimes recollected or reimagined a more relaxed, hospitable Olde England that had been displaced. So heathland around towns and cities became an increasingly popular subject precisely when, or after, it had been developed for suburban villas and pleasure grounds. Such pictures documented passing peasant ways of life – for example, grazing sheep or donkeys – but they also portrayed the natural as well as social history of such landscapes, their flora and fauna, and also their more atmospheric amenities, including bracing fresh air. Such qualities appealed to an urban population used to making excursions to the country, and now finding their informal public recreational grounds under threat.

Constable's paintings of Hampstead Heath convey this cultural moment. The artist moved permanently from central London to Hampstead in 1819 to establish a family home in a hilltop village famed for its healthy environment, its fresh air, clean water and nature walks. Hampstead also provided new subjects for his art, notably the expanses of heathland and big skies, and a local creative community, of literary and scientific minds, who shared the painter's investigative views of landscape. The connection to London is a theme of Constable's Hampstead pictures, shown as a green space for urban excursionists, and a foreground of panoramas of the smoky city. The heath is shown as a working environment, for grazing cattle and sheep, and as a place of gravel digging for building.

Above all, Hampstead provided an open-air laboratory for Constable's investigation of changing weather conditions, with hundreds of study sketches of skies, featuring cloud formations, showers and rainbows, annotated with times, dates and locations. These paralleled the observations of pioneering scientists of urban climate like Luke Howard, and Constable kept up to date with meteorological theory as well as day-to-day weather conditions. 'We see nothing truly till we understand it,' he declared, by which he meant the natural as well social world. 'Painting is a science and should be pursued as an inquiry into the laws of nature.' Constable's atmospheric investigations gave his landscapes a startling realistic power, as if spectators were experiencing the scenes in the gallery itself.

Constable's pictures of Hampstead Heath, rather than Suffolk, were the ones that first attracted Victorians. 'See how England rises before us in all her wealth of picturesque beauty', noted one influential critic in 1866, 'not clipped and cropped as the corn manufacturers disfigure her but English nature as it holds its own in our rude heaths and commons.' The year before, the Commons Preservation Society had been founded with the object of securing 'for the use and enjoyment of the public open spaces situated in the neighbourhood of towns, and especially of London'. One of its earliest campaigns was to fight the attempted enclosure of Hampstead Heath. Against the actual law of commons, and the interests of the main landowner, who wanted to sell land for building, they successfully promoted a myth of ancient rights of public access – which, said one official, 'had something of the attributes of ancient Saxon Folk-Land'. The campaign to secure Hampstead Heath for the public went on for years, as Constable's Heath pictures, and others inspired by them, rose in popularity. In 1871 the Hampstead Heath Act entrusted the Metropolitan Board of Works with the responsibility to 'for ever keep the Heath open, unenclosed and unbuilt on', much as it appears today.

Hills and Dales

Enclosure did not transform the landscape everywhere. While some places might already have been subject to earlier waves of enclosure by agreement, other places never saw enclosure at all, or if they did it came much later and had different effects.

Shunned as wild and unregulated, the open landscapes of the uplands came, gradually and over the course of the eighteenth century, to achieve a greater recognition as distinctive settings in their own right. This was mainly because they were seen as natural rather than social landscapes, sublimely wild, soaring peaks. Few travellers, however, dwelled upon the social significance of the open uplands, preferring to admire their scenic qualities as if they were God-given. Yet these upland landscapes were still the product of human interaction with the land, and as a matter of livelihood the practice of commoning often continued far longer than in lowland regions, as a consequence of the need to manage jointly the shared resource of the pasture grounds.

Below | Sheep graze the rocky slopes of Dovedale in Derbyshire. Dovedale is about 3 miles in length. Its most famous section is the wooded ravine between the famous stepping stones, laid across the River Dove circa 1890, and now owned by the National Trust.

Above | A legacy of upland hill farming, and a distinctive characteristic of the Yorkshire Dales, field barns or laithes were situated in hay meadows. Hay was stored on the first floor over the winter to feed the cattle sheltered on the floor below. The manure was used to fertilise the fields the following year.

Right | Farmhouse on the Dolmelynllyn Estate, Gwynedd. The estate is prime sheep-farming territory, with two tenanted farms, the spectacular Rhaeadr Ddu waterfall and traditional gold mines.

Pastoral myths of commons may mask some pastoral realities. There are still around 405,000 hectares (more than 1 million acres) of common land in England and Wales, most privately owned, much of it working country, grazing land, in upland regions of northern England and Wales. Within these areas there is rich diversity in the commons culture of landscape, their character and identity varying according to terrain, tradition, neighbourliness, custom, historical development and interaction with national legislation and designations that affect the land and its management. The long and continuing history of upland commons is rich and complicated, but often features much less in national narratives of landscape history than laments for lost lowland commons. The pioneering research gathered in the book *Contested Common Land* by Chris Rodgers and his team has transformed our understanding.

The development of Eskdale Common in Cumbria is an integral part of the valley's landscape history. Initially an aristocratic estate, it is now a more extensive, and highly

Above | Gathering the Welsh Mountain sheep on
Watkin Path on the Hafod Y Llan Farm, Snowdonia.

varied, National Trust estate that includes the highest mountain in England, Scafell Pike, and its deepest Lake, Wastwater, as well as the remains of the Roman fort high on Hardknott Pass, and the more tranquil river scenery of the Duddon Valley. Eskdale Common was owned for much of its history by the Earls of Northumberland and, latterly, by their successors the Lords Leconfield. Then, in 1979, it was transferred to the National Trust. This substantially increased the Trust's holdings in the valley. The freehold on the high fells was donated to the National Trust early in the century, the peaks, including that of Scafell Pike, as a memorial to Lakelanders who had died in the First World War. This forged a new meaning for commons, as an amenity of public access, the plaque on the summit announcing that it was 'subject to any commoners rights'. The National Trust remains committed to these common pasture lands, recognising that, along with farm tenancies it has acquired, they form a vital part of Eskdale as a working environment.

Until the later nineteenth century, the management of common rights in Eskdale was regulated by a manor court, with a jury of local customary tenants making and enforcing agrarian rules. The common then entered a period without a management institution, until the formation of a commoners committee in 1945. This was largely the creation of a conservationist campaigner, the Reverend H. H. Symonds, who was prominent in national pressure groups for public access to the countryside. It lapsed when Symonds moved away from the locality, and the gap was filled in 1967 by a more successful body that was endorsed by the landowner but which had more significant grassroots support from the commoners. The Eskdale Commoners Association was formed primarily to prepare for the registration of rights under the Commons Registration Act of 1965, and it continues now as a vehicle of collective action.

Commons pasture, mainly for sheep, remains central to hill farming and livelihood, though turbary and estovers have now fallen into disuse given the use of alternative sources for fuel, roofing and animal bedding. Their legacy in the landscape takes the form of the remains of peat tracks and huts (some rerofed) and the rampant spread of bracken. The landscape also reveals remains of former landowners' rights on the common – to game, in the form of grouse butts and hunting lodges; and to minerals, in the form of the ruined mine workings and the narrow-gauge track of a former mineral railway that once transported iron ore and granite to the port of Ravenglass. In the mid-twentieth century this railway promoted local tourism, bringing in visitors from the industrial Cumbrian coast, including the poet Norman Nicholson. His writings on Eskdale, in poems and guidebooks, did much to enhance the appreciation of Eskdale as an enterprising, working country, governed by its sturdy 'statesmen' farmers:

Above | Herdwick sheep at Wastwater in Cumbria. Herdwicks are the native breed of the central and western Lake District. They are extremely hardy, grazing on fells of over 900 metres.

Above | Bird How is a National Trust holiday cottage that is situated on the fellside above the River Esk at the head of Eskdale.

Left | Wasdale Head from the foot of Kirk Fell, Cumbria. Lake District farms tend to have an area of privately owned or managed land in the valley bottoms, divided by dry-stone walls, and large areas of commonly grazed fell land.

... The ESK comes from the narrowest dale
Where the statesmen meet at the Woolpack for a glass of ale
And a crack about Herdwicks or a cure for the tick
And how some fool has broken his neck on the rock.

Common rights in Eskdale were codified by a document originally drawn up in 1587 and known as the 'Eskdale Twenty-Four Book', so-called because it was prepared by a jury of 24 men. No less than estate maps and account books of the period, the Book was part of a new, modern, rational framework of land management, precisely prescribing and demarcating the time and space for commons practice. For pasture, the Book designated each commoner's heaf (grazing portion of the fell) and drift (the designated route to it), conceiving the common in terms of grazing capacity and taking into account the different livestock (sheep, cattle, horses), topography and ground cover, thus creating a patchwork of practices. The book has proved sufficiently flexible to accommodate four centuries of economic and social change, including the

development of Eskdale for industry and tourism and the transfer of government from the manor to other institutions. No original copy of the book is known, but it has been periodically copied and transcribed – in relation to stocking disputes, for example. It continued to be consulted as a framework for commons governance long after the manor court's demise and into the twentieth century, in conjunction with more recent texts, including legal statutes of modern environmental stewardship on grazing strategy as well as new fell rules drawn up in 1980 by the Association when the National Trust acquired ownership.

The Twenty-Four Book deserves to be better known, not only as an enduring framework for commons governance, one that has been adapted and appropriated through a long history of practical use, but also for its language of landscape. One passage concerns 'the tenants of Spouthouse':

We find that they shall take their sheep up their bank or bankedge and on the south side of Bleatarne upon their accustomed waye upon the height of Brownband and up over the How of Swinside and up at Eile Ark to the Hardrigge and if their sheep be on the north side of Bleatarn that then they shall take them and go to their drift both at cominge and going there at will and pleasure.

Here is a language of landscape that emphasises movement and process, through a detailed topography of named places and pathways. It finds its echoes in the literature of the Lake District, sensitive to places like Eskdale off the beaten track and mindful of their forgotten ways.

Commons in Trust

Commons have not disappeared entirely from lowland England. They have followed a different evolutionary path, often involving the transformation of specific common rights into more general public rights, usually associated with questions of access and recreation. At Brancaster and Thornham on the North Norfolk coast, for example, the nature and purpose of common land has been subject to a far greater degree of reinterpretation over time compared to that in Eskdale. Ironically, it was enclosure in the eigtheenth century that effectively created the commons here, formalising them as such when the open heath was otherwise parcelled up and allotted to private owners.

A wider variety of common rights were also practised here, reflecting the varied products of this coastal landscape. Rights to collect samphire, shellfish and wildfowl were among those recorded following the Commons Registration Act of 1965, which attempted to achieve some measure of regularity over the vastly complex pattern of surviving commons at that time. Rights such as these were, strictly, customary rather than common; nonetheless, the legal processes of enclosure and then of commons registration provided moments for reinterpreting and reinventing the meaning of common land.

The National Trust, which now owns and looks after the very different commons at both Eskdale and at Brancaster, was born when the pressures of industrialisation led to a quite radical new approach to the protection of landscape. The Trust was established as a property-owning body, but one that was to hold land on behalf of the nation. This was a highly innovative solution to a problem widely acknowledged as urgent and pressing: the urbanisation of Britain and the sprawl of towns and cities over areas of highly valued open country.

While protest groups like the Commons Preservation Society had fought battles in the 1860s and 1870s to protect areas like Wimbledon Common, Epping Forest and Hampstead Heath from development, they were only ever able to exert at most a

Right | Boat moored on the intertidal mudflats at Brancaster Staithe on the north Norfolk coast.

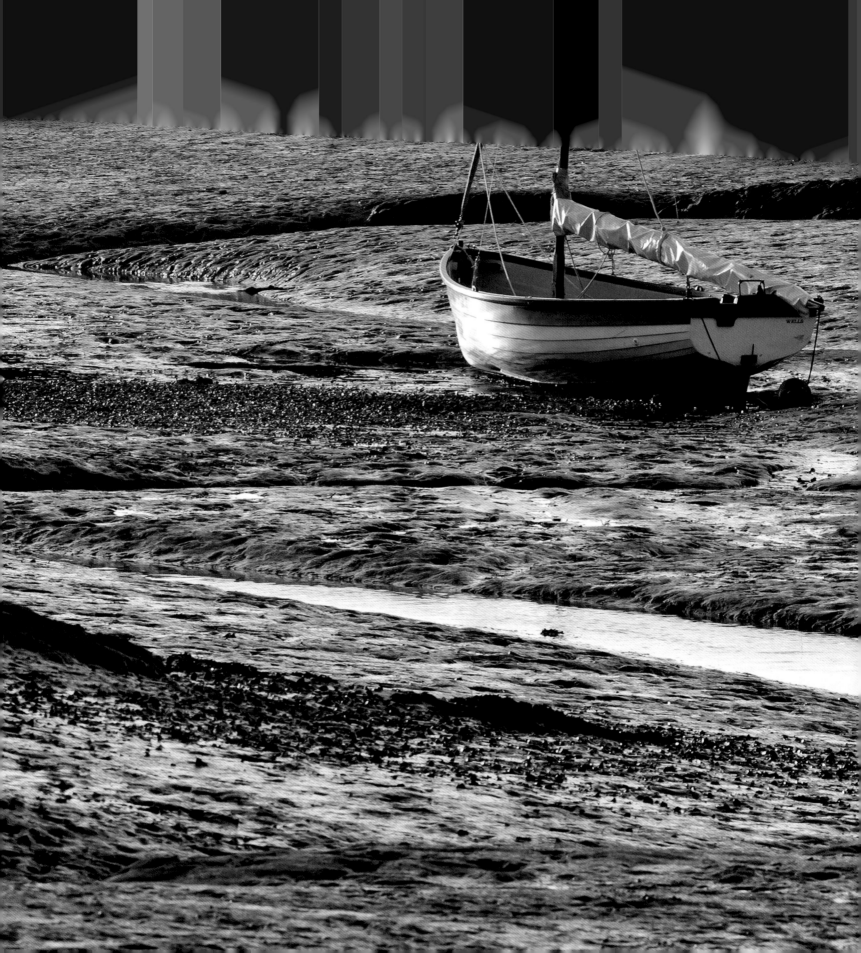

regulatory influence. They were not able to acquire such lands directly from their owners and to conserve them for public use. The National Trust was established to do just that, consciously following the example set by the Massachusetts Trustees of Reservation in 1891. Robert Hunter, Solicitor to the Commons Preservation Society, was the inspiration behind the idea, having proposed a few years earlier that some sort of land company would be needed in order to promote 'the better preservation of open spaces'.

Octavia Hill proposed 'The Commons and Gardens Trust' as a name for the venture, but it was the 'National Trust' that became established as a private charitable company in 1895. It was given greater status and import as a consequence of its incorporation into the statute book through the National Trust Act of 1907, which gave the Trust its powers to hold land inalienably on behalf of the nation – meaning that, once acquired, the land could not be sold or otherwise released without explicit Parliamentary approval.

Many of the Trust's earliest acquisitions were of open landscapes and countryside, reflecting the ambitions of Octavia Hill for 'places to sit in, places to play in, places to stroll in, and places to spend a day in'. Spiritual and social concerns commingled in the ideas of the Trust's founders. As hinted by her very name, Octavia Hill was a devotee of the uplands, using the elevation gained from an uphill walk to get closer to God and creation. While the Trust acquired much common land, and now looks after more than one-tenth of the surviving commons in England and Wales, this acquisition was part of the process in the second half of the nineteenth century whereby common landscapes became public resources, available to all. Public access was the driving ambition, seeking to ensure that open landscapes like the Devil's Punch Bowl in Surrey, which was acquired by the Trust in 1906, were managed essentially for recreation and delight. The recent re-routing of a section of the busy A3 trunk road from London to Portsmouth through a tunnel beneath the Devil's Punch Bowl represents merely the latest victory for those seeking to protect open countryside as a public amenity. And this time, it was the technological advances associated with enlightened modern transport infrastructure that made this possible.

Below | People walking their dogs along the old A3 main road, now grassed over, at the Devil's Punch Bowl, Hindhead Commons in Surrey.

Right | A family enjoying the view just below the viewpoint at the Devil's Punch Bowl, Hindhead Commons, Surrey.

Landscape-scale Conservation

The National Trust was established in order to protect landscapes for future generations, including places of both natural importance and historical significance. Since the Trust's foundation, however, the crisis facing nature has become even more acute. With the loss of so many species from our countryside, it is clear that caring for places in isolation from their context is insufficient as a response. Only by looking after entire landscapes, at scale, can the conditions be created in which nature can once again thrive. Increasingly the Trust is working with tenant farmers and other partners to promote better ways to manage land.

Above | Wicken Fen was one of the first nature reserves acquired by the National Trust. More than a century later, the Wicken Vision looks to expand the area managed as fen, creating a wetland landscape that will ultimately stretch as far as the edge of the city of Cambridge.

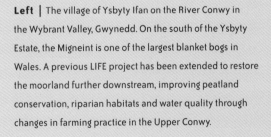

Left | The village of Ysbyty Ifan on the River Conwy in the Wybrant Valley, Gwynedd. On the south of the Ysbyty Estate, the Migneint is one of the largest blanket bogs in Wales. A previous LIFE project has been extended to restore the moorland further downstream, improving peatland conservation, riparian habitats and water quality through changes in farming practice in the Upper Conwy.

Above | The Trust is working with farmers and others to create habitats and promote access along the South West coast. This picture shows wild asparagus growing along the coastline near Cadgwith, the Lizard, Cornwall.

Above | Ennerdale Valley in the Lake District National Park, Cumbria, has some of England's most vibrant uplands landscapes. The Wild Ennerdale Partnership is one of a number of initiatives promoting sustainable land management across the Lakes, helping to restore nature and a sense of wilderness.

Left | St Margaret's church on the Felbrigg Estate. In the Bure Valley, which joins up two National Trust properties (Felbrigg and Blickling) a project is underway to achieve improvements across the catchment in lowland farming practices, riparian habitats and floodplain management.

Above | The High Peak Moors stretch over almost 40 square miles of the Peak District National Park, spanning the high ground between Manchester and Sheffield. They cover boulder-strewn landscapes of rocky tors, dramatic hanging valleys and cloughs, and mile upon mile of wild and remote bog.

Left | On the South Downs, work is under way to improve land quality and conserve landscape character. Landscape-scale networks create habitats that encourage species (such as rare bats) to thrive. This is the view looking towards Newtimber Hill at Devil's Dyke, South Downs, West Sussex.

Chapter 6

Shifting Shores

Worth their salt, England's white cliffs;
a glittering breastplate
Caesar saw from his ship;
the sea's gift to the land,
where samphire-pickers hung from their long ropes,
gathering, under a gull-glad sky,
in Shakespeare's mind's eye;
astonishing
 in Arnold's glimmering verse;
marvellous geology, geography;
to time, deference; war, defence;
first view or last of here, home,
in painting, poem, play, in song;
something fair and strong implied in chalk,
what we might wish ourselves.

'White Cliffs', Carol Ann Duffy

This poem, by the Poet Laureate Carol Ann Duffy, was commissioned by the National Trust to mark the success of its appeal to purchase one of the last stretches of the White Cliffs of Dover still in private ownership. The speed and spread of the appeal's success – months ahead of the deadline, securing £1.2 million from more than 16,000 individuals and organisations in just 133 days – is a measure of the value of the White Cliffs as a national landmark. The Trust appointed a philosopher-in-residence as part of the appeal, recalling those 'hermits' hired in the eighteenth century to perform the role of oracles in picturesque sites, or at least to look the part.

Among the celebrities supporting the appeal was Dame Vera Lynn, herself now a national treasure, whose 1942 recording of the song '(There'll be Bluebirds Over) The White Cliffs of Dover' became both a hit song and patriotic anthem. While the American songwriters had never seen the famous cliffs, nor blue birds ever flown over them, the lyrics effectively created an image of transatlantic union for a cross-channel European conflict, a special relationship which ensured that American popular opinion would back an allied war effort and that American war planes would fly over the cliffs of England alongside British ones.

Left | Aerial view of land on the White Cliffs of Dover stretch of coastline in Kent, which the National Trust was able to acquire following a successful appeal in 2012.

Previous page | Sand dunes and marram grass at Blakeney Point in Norfolk. The National Nature Reserve at Blakeney is a combination of saltmarsh and dunes within a curving sand and shingle spit that is vulnerable to tidal action and storms.

Duffy's poem alludes to the long history of the cliffs' 'marvellous geology, geography ... in painting, poem, play, in song', as a matter of both hope and loss, the first and last view of the nation, a place of invasion as well as a line of defence. Duffy references the fragile qualities of this soft chalk face, the samphire pickers clinging to it in Shakespeare's *King Lear* and the eternal note of sadness in Mathew Arnold's 'glimmering verse' of Victorian religious doubt, 'Dover Beach'. Meanwhile the plaintive appeal of Vera Lynn's record was the barely concealed heartache within its fair hope for the future. The coast as an emblem of national identity has long combined strength and vulnerability, its confident rocky cliff faces lined by the shifting shores of doubt and insecurity.

The chalk cliffs at Dover, indeed all along the southern coast, have been constantly changing, in response to both natural and human forces. Rock falls are commonplace and built structures gradually approach the edge. Perhaps more than most places, the coast reminds us that landscape is in a permanent state of physical change, both gradual and long term. Variations on geological timescales confront the more immediate challenges of environmental change in the here and now – as a result of rising sea levels, for example.

The full stretch of White Cliffs now owned by the National Trust, more than 4 miles long, is the latest piece in a long history of coastal acquisition and conservation. The very first piece of land owned by the newly formed Trust, in 1895, was a coastal property, the bequest of a rocky outcrop of land known as Dinas Oleu above Barmouth in North Wales. In the face of increasing pressures on the coast in the mid-twentieth century, the result of unbridled seaside development or neglect and decline, the Trust launched its Neptune Campaign in 1965, named after the Roman God of the Sea. The Trust now owns 742 miles of coastline, one-tenth of the total length in England, Wales and Northern Ireland. Nowhere in Britain is more than 46½ miles from the coast and the pressures for public access to shoreline scenery, along with that of the rivers that flow into them, is increasing. The 2009 Marine and Coastal Access Act gave the government agency Natural England the authority to create a walking route around the coast of England. This has been an ambition of recreation and countryside groups since 1949 and the aim is to complete it by 2020.

Right | Coastguard cottages at Birling Gap, East Sussex, move ever closer to the edge as the sea undermines the Seven Sisters cliff range.

Left | Dinas Oleu, a small gorse-covered stretch of fell, seen from Barmouth Beach, Gwynedd, was the first acquisition of the National Trust.

The coast is an increasing focus of national concern, both social and environmental. Flooding and future scenarios of sea levels rising offer environmental challenges while the present rise of second-home ownership in well-to-do resorts is a social challenge, as is the concentration of benefit claimants in declining resorts. The past life and legends of the coast come into focus, especially those times when it was a key zone of production and communication as well as a gateway to a global empire. Natural changes can reveal human landscapes of the past, such as the 2013 storm surge on the east coast of England, which both damaged the delicate ecosystem at Orford Ness and excavated some of its history as a port settlement.

As the coast and its complex, changeful nature is opened up to the public, so all agencies, including the Trust, must devise new approaches. It is a challenge to cope with social and natural pressures, from surfers and fishermen to storms and floods, and with the number of different contact zones between land and water, including cliff faces, harbours, riverbanks, and estuaries.

Below | Weathered and damaged wooden groynes, part of the failed coastal defence at Bossington Beach, a shingle bar on the Holnicote Estate, North Somerset.

Neptune and After

The National Trust's very first property, Dinas Oleu outside Barmouth in Wales, was a coastal site, and the Trust has continued to acquire stretches of coastline ever since. The Trust's 70th anniversary year in 1965 saw the launch of the Neptune Campaign, to raise funds for acquiring and looking after threatened coastal sites. It proved the most successful campaign in the Trust's history, which itself speaks to the nation's abiding love affair with the sea. The Trust now looks after almost 750 miles of coastline, and welcomes millions of visitors every year to its coastal properties, which include beaches, cliff-tops, rocky promontories and low-lying saltmarshes.

Above | Acquired in 1966, Dunwich Heath and Beach in Suffolk is part of an Area of Outstanding Natural Beauty, and adjoins the Minsmere Reserve. It provides a rare example of coastal heather heathland, supporting a rich diversity of wildlife. The dynamic nature of this stretch of the Suffolk coast means that the medieval town of Dunwich, once a prosperous port, was completely lost to the sea.

Above | Looking out across Rhossili Bay, Gower in Wales, a Neptune site since 1967. Rhossili is part of the first ever Area of Outstanding Natural Beauty to be designated in the UK. Now popular with tourists and surfers, the area contains prehistoric remains as well as a number of shipwrecks on the beach.

Right | A view over The Needles on the far western point of the Isle of Wight, owned by the National Trust since 1975. This unusual formation of three chalk stacks takes its name from a fourth rock, which was needle-shaped and toppled into the sea in the eighteenth century.

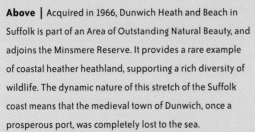

Left | A view across a rippled sandy beach at Whiteford Burrows, Gower Peninsula, Wales. This was the first Neptune site acquired by the National Trust. The dunes here back Whiteford Sands, and are classified as a National Nature Reserve. Its tranquillity and biodiversity today belies a past of industrial and agricultural exploitation.

Left | Five hectares (12 acres) of Robin Hood's Bay was acquired in 1976. This view is taken from Rocket Post Field, just north of Robin Hood's Bay town. The field derives its name from the posts that were used for practising the rescue of ships by firing rockets with ropes attached. Ravenscar occupies the distant southern headland.

Left | Stackpole Quay, Pembrokeshire, Wales. Eight miles around Stackpole came under the care of the National Trust in 1976. This remote spot is an internationally important nature reserve. Stackpole Quay itself is a tiny harbour used by local fishermen and small pleasure boats. Nearby, Barafundle Bay provides an untouched stretch of beach, while Bosherston Lakes have evolved into a wildlife habitat famous for otters, water birds and dragonflies.

Below | Rocky foreshore at Wembury Point, near Plymouth, Devon, acquired from the Ministry of Defence in 2004. The Great Mewstone lies in the distance. The rocks here contribute to the wide diversity of plant and animal life on Wembury Point, which enjoys multiple forms of environmental protection. The area is noted for having one of the largest populations of shore dock in Devon, for example.

Above | The Souter Lighthouse at Marsden, Tyne and Wear was acquired in 1990. The coastline here was among the most treacherous in the country. The lighthouse opened in 1871 and was the first purpose-built to use alternating electric current. It was decommissioned in 1988.

Island Nation

The old idea of Britain as an island nation strengthened when that geographical image became political reality with the union of the crowns of England and Scotland in 1603. Great Britain, as it was called, became the only major European nation state that could claim to have no borders but the ocean. 'Rule Britannia', composed in 1740, was one of many lyrics to insist that the nation's imperial claim to rule the waves was a natural, even divinely ordained one, Britain arising 'out of the sea at heaven's command'. The timber required to build the nation's military and merchant navy, particularly the oak woods needed for large war ships, extended the naturalistic image of the nation, connecting land and sea. Sturdy sailors had 'hearts of oak', and on the high seas the navy's ships comprised the 'wooden walls' of the nation.

In the face of serious threats to Britain and its maritime power from rival imperial states, notably invasion from Napoleonic France around the turn of the eighteenth century, this image hardened in patriotic heart and minds. In 1803, the French navy blockaded the Channel and massed 115,000 troops at Boulogne, who were visible to people strolling the south coast with portable telescopes. An English cartoon showed a strutting if diminutive Napoleon in outsize Corsican boots looking across at John Bull, who was sitting on a white cliff beneath an oak tree, smoking. The image of a nonchalant John Bull belied the acute anxieties of invasion at the time.

Above | Two 12-tonne guns on iron carriages in gun emplacements at the Needles Old Battery on the far western point of the Isle of Wight. The Old Battery is a Victorian fort, built in 1861–63 following the threat of a French invasion, to protect the approaches to the Needles Passage.

Left | 'Conversation across the Water', a satirical print published by Piercy Roberts in London 1803–04. John Bull threatens, '… if you attempt to stir a foot – there's a few of my wooden walls in the offing shall give you a pretty peppering.'

CONVERSATION across the WATER

Above | Trewavas Cliff in Cornwall, part of the Cornish Mining World Heritage Site, with the impressive and precarious remains of Wheal Trewavas copper mine.

The Battle of Trafalgar in 1805 began the Allied command of the ocean and by 1812, with Napoleon camped outside Moscow and focused on a land war in Europe, there was growing confidence in the nation's coastal security. Tourists flocked to the coast, and artists accompanied them, charting the impressive fortifications, ancient and modern, which had faced invaders. Among them were old castles and bastions as well as modern Martello towers and moored warships. Similarly there was a flourishing livelihood along the coasts – the beaches, harbours and ports for fishing and trade; the smart new villas of seasonal and permanent residents; the shoreline tin mines of Cornwall and coal mines of Northumberland; the cliff-top fields and pastures along the southern coast – and this, as well as other natural historical wonders, both geological and botanical, revealed where the land met the sea.

Humphry Repton's 1812 design for the coastal estate of Sheringham in Norfolk presents the landscape as the epitome of the nation at large. With its outlook tower to scan the horizon for signs of invasion, the property was originally envisaged as a landscape park called Trafalgar, to be given by a grateful nation to the family of Norfolkman Admiral Lord Nelson, one of a number of coastal memorials created at this time. As it turned out, he would be commissioned by private clients, though the brief was still to create a landscape with public, patriotic associations.

Repton's clients, a passionate young couple called Abbot and Charlotte Upcher, were East Anglian but took inspiration for their new home from a seaside holiday on the Isle of Wight, with its famous coastal views. Mindful of Sheringham's chilly, north-facing aspect, Repton designed a landscape that offered shelter from storms, both social and natural, and which faced both landward and seaward. A hill-top temple, open to the public, offered panoramic views of the sea, thronged with coastal shipping as a result of Sheringham's position between the ports of Blakeney and Cromer.

Now silted up and a National Trust nature reserve, Blakeney was an important centre of European trade, exporting grain and importing timber, furs and iron.

267

Cromer was a flourishing fishing port and a centre of the new seaside industry, as well as an anchorage for war ships on breaks from duties off the coasts of Scandinavia.

Repton's view of the beach at Sheringham was a public one showing a hare-coursing match. In the early nineteenth century, this was the kind of entertainment which, like cricket, encouraged all social ranks to mix. Indeed the beach scene offered an emblematic image of social harmony, if a momentary, tidal one, a littoral landscape between landward aristocratic British power and the democratic forces from across the ocean. Repton himself wrote:

Smooth as the Level Sand 'twixt Land and Sea
So may our middle Course of Life run free
Twixt overwhelming Power, and mad Equality

The temple Repton proposed also offered a view of the woods of Sheringham, including its sturdy oaks – battered but unbowed by North Sea gales, just as Britain's wooden walls and hearts of oak had proved so many times in the past. In his words, 'England's oaks resist the sea, emblem of strength, increased by unity.' So panoramic was the view from the temple that his verse has the gods dispute its dedication to Neptune, with Pan, Flora and Diana claiming it for forestry, horticulture and hunting respectively, Venus claiming it for the love of the young couple and Bacchus for the refreshment of tourists. The death of Abbot Upcher in 1819 meant, though, that the temple was never

built. In 1975, the Upcher family did add one to the estate but in a different place to that suggested by Repton.

The sea view today is no longer animated by ships but by those new emblems of wind-powered energy, offshore wind turbines. Such industrial-scale development within the vicinity of one of the most complete of Repton's designs to survive on the ground today seems jarring, although perhaps it is not altogether out of keeping given Repton's regard for cliff-top windmills in his design.

People in the early nineteenth century were well aware of the shifting shores of Sheringham. Its cliffs were made of soft and varied materials that had a low resistance, making them vulnerable to wave erosion and land slips through undercutting. Repton himself observed on an earlier visit that

Lower Sheringham is situated on a part of the cliff which is but a few yards from the beach, and the cliff gradually rises on each side to upwards of a hundred; the sea gains considerably here, and it is not uncommon to observe large pieces of arable land carried away with corn growing, betwixt feed time and harvest so near do the people plough to the edge of a cliff, which strikes a stranger with horror to look down it.

Above | The location of the temple is slightly to the north of Repton's design, in order for it to command an uninterrupted view across the park to the Hall and the sea beyond.

A visit to Sheringham inspired the pioneering geologist Charles Lyell to publish in 1830 his *Principles of Geology*, a book that popularised James Hutton's concept of 'uniformitarianism', the theory that the earth is shaped by slow-moving processes which are still in operation. Lyell's measurement of coastal retreat at Sheringham emphasised the continual operation of change under natural forces.

Between the years 1824 and 1829, no less than seventeen yards were swept away, and only a small garden was then left between the building and the sea. There is now a depth of twenty feet (sufficient to float a frigate) at one point in the harbour of that port, where, only forty-eight years ago, there stood a cliff fifty feet high, with houses upon it! If once in half a century an equal amount of change were produced at once by the momentary shock of an earthquake, history would be filled with records of such wonderful revolutions of the earth's surface, but, if the conversion of high land into deep sea be gradual, it excites only local attention.

For Charles Dickens, geological lectures featuring material like Lyell's prompted alarm, through an unpleasant realisation that the earth was still evolving. Dickens supposed that there might once have been three Sheringhams, one of which lay at the bottom of the sea. His supposition appears to have been partly prompted by personal observations of coastal retreat at Sheringham, where groynes were being constructed to combat loss. As he wrote in the magazine *Household Words*,

They say that the original Lower Sheringham is now at the bottom of the sea. If this be really true, as it doubtless is, then there are three, not two Sheringhams, to be distinguished, according to the three degrees of comparison, as Upper Sheringham, Lower Sheringham, and Lowest Sheringham. Unhappy trio! What is to become of you?

Above | View of Weybourne chalk cliffs from the headland at Sheringham Park in Norfolk. This stretch of coastline is a productive site for fossil finds in fresh cliff falls.

Victorians flocked to the coast by steamboat and train for serious speculations on nature and culture, as well as for seaside holiday fun. Visitors to respectable resorts (like Ramsgate) often marked their distance from the denizens of rougher, more frolicsome neighbours (like Margate) by setting out on high-minded excursions along the shore, to exercise their minds and bodies. 'The point where the land and sea meet is the critical point for all observers of nature,' noted Henry Eley, the author of a popular book on pebbles. *Geology in the Garden or, The Fossils in the Flint Pebbles* (1959) was aimed at middle-class visitors keen on beachcombing – an appropriate ladies' pursuit.

William Dyce's painting *Pegwell Bay – A Recollection of October 5th 1858* is a sublime, earth-shaking image of a quiet, everyday event. The picture shows a party of Victorian women and girls from the nearby town of Ramsgate exploring the shore, collecting specimens, gathering pebbles and shells and peering into rockpools, the whole scene shown in the microscopic detail that characterised popular scientific vision itself. The flint-encrusted strata of the white chalk cliffs are shown buckled by ancient earth

Above | William Dyce, *Pegwell Bay – A Recollection of October 5th 1858*, oil on canvas, Tate.

movements and eroded by modern ones, with scooped-out hollows and overhanging turf and soil – in a site which, Lyell noted, had lost three feet per annum over the last ten years. The fossil shells in the chalk attested that the dry land was formerly an ocean bed, and challenged biblical chronologies of the earth. Dead centre of the composition, streaking across the dusky sky, is the arc of a new astronomical sight, Donati's Comet, reputed to be the largest and brightest comet ever seen at the date of the painting and provoking a range of speculations in the press on interplanetary space. A small stretch of shoreline is shown in the sublime immensity of time and space. The junction between sea and land, and the great vistas it offers, prompt reflections on the profoundest questions, the junction between religion and science, between secular and spiritual vision.

Meanwhile, the crowds in Margate found lighter entertainments, larking around on the sands and flocking to the end of the pier. Like many Londoners, J. M. W. Turner was a regular visitor to the resort, taking one of the many paddle steamers down the Thames. In watercolours, a medium that suited his subject, he depicted the shifting states of the seaside, waves and tides, clouds and rain, the social cross-currents of bathers and fishermen, the offshore mêlée of fishing boats and pleasure boats, coastal collier brigs from the North East and cross-channel packets. These were all vessels which showed in a landscape what the eye could not see: the ocean as an energetic system of commerce

Below | J. M. W. Turner, *The New Moon; or 'I've Lost My Boat, You Shan't Have Your Hoop'*, exhibited in 1840, oil on mahogany, Tate.

Above | Kayaking past Old Harry Rocks, the chalk stacks on the Purbeck coast that mark the eastern end of the Jurassic Coast.

and exchange, a network of towns and nations. A continental traveller, Turner was one of those English artists who acknowledged that the Channel had two sides. During the wars he showed the implications of the blockade for the southern English coast, scenes of smuggling and the dumping of pilchards once exported to France, and afterwards he depicted the shores of northern France, the commerce and history of Calais and Dieppe.

The artistic allure of the coast has been revived in new programmes of heritage interpretation and cultural creativity. Ramsgate and Margate, as shown by Dyce and Turner, offer two contemporary models of coastal heritage and cultural regeneration. The high-minded image of Pegwell Bay is reflected in the interpretation and management of the Jurassic Coast of Dorset and East Devon. This World Heritage Site takes its name from a nineteenth-century geological term for the period of earth history revealed in its strata, while also alluding to the modern cult of fossils and dinosaurs and the 1993 science-fiction film *Jurassic Park*. Visitors are guided on a 'walk through time': here is an outdoor theatre for learning about the art and science of coastal change, for charting stories of the complex relations between nature and culture, between society and stratigraphy.

At Margate, Turner's name has been enlisted for a different style of cultural regeneration. With the vocal backing of Britart bad girl Tracey Emin, a Margate native, the new Turner Contemporary Gallery is a landmark in a programme of regeneration for a rundown resort. While the gallery is part of the 'creative quarter' in the Old Town, with the narrow lanes and cottages to attract well-heeled visitors and second-home owners, it is also meant to renovate the playful seaside traditions of 'Merry Margate', including its amusement parks. Similar culture-led regeneration projects on the southern coast can be seen at places such as Folkestone and Bexhill, where the creative possibilities of coastal vistas are drawn into artists' practice. The Folkestone Triennial is one example, taking place at various vantage points along the once highly fashionable Edwardian promenades.

Left | Looking up at the distinctive layers of Bridport Sands that make up Burton Cliff on the Jurassic Coast, Dorset.

Estuary England

The soft, low-lying shores of the Thames Estuary and adjoining coasts have long been the subject of military control – with fortification, garrisoning and communications to secure this gateway to the national capital. These monuments are the marks of successive wars and invasion threats. The remains of Roman forts, medieval castles, Martello towers, the pill boxes and radar stations of the Second World War, and the weapons testing laboratories and bunkers of the Cold War all leave their traces on this landscape, as do the fully functioning, operational structures of the current Defence establishment, off limits to the visiting public. If this is a patriotic landscape, it is a paranoid one.

Sited at the very edge of the coast, on shingle and reclaimed marshland, jutting out into the sea, military and former military sites contribute to the haunting air of mystery, of danger and desolation, which has shrouded this estuary region, so near and yet so far from the densely developed landscapes of London and the South East.

Just beyond the seaside fun of Southend-on-Sea is the eerie expanse of MOD Shoeburyness, a permanently restricted zone used for the development and evaluation of weapons and the decommissioning of unstable and out-of-date incendiaries. Its silence is 'almost supernaturally enhanced' by unusual birdcalls, droning insects, sweeping wind, and the occasional blasts and thuds of exploding shells.

Left | View across the saltmarsh and meandering creeks of Copt Hall Marshes in the Blackwater Estuary on the Essex coast.

Below | The partly submerged causeway across the Blackwater Estuary that connects Northey Island to mainland Essex. The island is always cut off at high tide.

In the middle of Foulness, the 'secret island' of this military-scientific complex, is a farming village dating back to medieval times, now an Area of Special Architectural and Historic Interest, with a heritage centre. Today it is more isolated than ever by the closure of former roads, the demolition of outlying buildings and the closure of the village pub, hall and primary school. And yet, life goes on, the villagers ploughing and harvesting fields that double as firing ranges, working in and around the military planning schedule, and there is much less local complaint within Shoeburyness about noise and inconvenience than there is from the gentrified villages outside. The military-scientific exclusion zone extends beyond the fields, marshes and sands to the sea and sky, reaching 26 miles out into the North Sea, and it is closed to civilian aircraft and shipping in the daylight hours of the working week.

Further north, beyond the container port of Felixstowe, on a long shingle spit, lies Orford Ness, now owned by the National Trust. A National Nature Reserve of considerable significance, Orford Ness is also managed for its military past, which adds to the aura of this landscape on the edge of England. Writers and artists drawn to such 'edgelands', are following, even if unwittingly, in the tracks of W. G. Sebald. In his influential psycho-travel book *The Rings of Saturn*, Sebald describes reaching Orford Ness and discovering a strange terrain that is always shifting and covering tracks, and which is highly exposed to the natural forces of time and tide.

Controlled access to Orford Ness by the ferry *Octavia*, which is named after the Trust's co-founder, conserves the sense of the place's special, clandestine atmosphere, with

the gothic frisson of its secret military past. Orford Ness is effectively landscaped with ruined structures and programmed with old remains and contemporary artworks – the 'pagodas' for atomic weapons testing (accessible for special events only); the signs warning of unexploded ordinance; the installations and performance works commissioned by the Trust to interpret the landscape. Decommissioned structures form ruined monuments to meditate on past military campaigns, including memento mori to global war.

Landscape researcher Matthew Flintham has pointed out that 'the military-pastoral complex' has been revived as a genre of landscape art on Orford Ness. Until the twentieth century, the military was more visible in the civilian landscape: troops were billeted among the population and trained on common land, royal parks or private estates, and they gave frequent public parade. Likewise, the apparatus of barracks and beacons, naval docks and anchorages were part of a wider landscape, as symbols of homeland security. In the twentieth century, the development of large defence establishment estates – with their extensive living quarters and firing ranges, as well as sites for intelligence gathering and weapons testing – securely segregated the military from the civil domain. This activated a pastorally patriotic version of rural landscape, which was suspicious or hostile to the military as symbols of unaccountable state power, particularly in the period of the Cold War. This is evident in twentieth-century writing, from science fiction like *The Midwich Cuckoos* to W.G. Hoskins' *The Making of the English Landscape* and activist imagery against nuclear weapons bases, such as the punning campaign slogan 'England's Greenham Pleasant Land'.

Right | Sir Robert Watson-Watt's Radar Tower at Orford Ness. The site conducted the first experiments into radar during the 1930s

Below | The 'Street' of derelict buildings running parallel to Stony Ditch on the north-east side of Orford Ness.

The National Trust

DANGER

UNEXPLODED ORDNANCE

PLEASE KEEP TO
THE VISITOR ROUTE

With the end of the Cold War, the military has raised its profile in public life. In part this is a public relations initiative (which includes the promotion of effective nature conservation on its estates), but it also reflects political pressures for more open access to state information, and the revival of public mourning for casualties of wars, including the spontaneous roadside ritual for the returning war dead in the village of Wootton Bassett. The landscape of Orford Ness has been the site of a creative, if still critically edged, cultural engagement, a new version of the military-pastoral complex.

Drawing on extensive research on Cold War architecture and technology, the artist Louise K. Wilson undertook a series of performances and artworks, collectively known as *A Record of Fear*, at Orford Ness in 2005. The decommissioned and decaying Atomic Weapons Research Establishment laboratories provided the subject and the venue for a number of sound works. Lab 2 is a building semi-submerged under a drift of shingle, which once housed an enormous centrifuge used for environmentally testing free-fall nuclear weapon casings. Here, Wilson installed two large infra-bass sub-woofer speakers. She also managed to gain access to AWE Aldermaston in Berkshire and recorded the sound of the same centrifuge used in Lab 2 during tests (which had been relocated to Aldermaston after the closure of Orford Ness).

Played back in the cylindrical central room, the throbbing, cycling, cardiac pulse of the weapon as it reaches one hundred revolutions per minute is 'the sound of a machine simultaneously present and absent; an echo of the past that is incontrovertibly present'. The auditory possibilities of this isolated and otherwise uncommunicative military complex were pushed further when Wilson persuaded a chamber choir, the Exmoor Singers, to perform at the site. In the control room adjacent to the 'pagoda' laboratories, the singers gathered around the casing of a WE177A free-fall nuclear bomb still on its loading trolley, and sang John Ward's Elizabethan madrigal of unrequited love 'Come Sable Night', transforming it into 'a lament for an age of pre-nuclear innocence'.

The Trust maintains a policy of 'controlled ruination' on Orford Ness, reminiscent of traditional landscaping strategies of picturesque decay. Yet such a policy challenges conventional understanding of heritage protection. The landmark lighthouse on Orford Ness, now in private ownership, was designed by architect William Wilkins and built in 1792 to aid navigation and warn ships of the treacherous coast. Although a beautiful Grade II listed building, it faces an uncertain future as a consequence of the erosion of the shingle spit on which it stands. There is no easy solution for 'saving' a lighthouse that now stands less than 8 metres from the sea, although the trust now responsible for it continues to explore different options for how its life might be extended and celebrated.

Warplands

Looking north on a still day, from the sparsely populated low hills of Lincolnshire at Alkborough to the great expanse of the Humber Estuary, nothing dramatic appears to be happening. Stay awhile and the slow movements of the tide become apparent: the wheeling and flocking of birds over the mudflats, or perhaps the steady course of a barge or tanker. These are the surface rhythms of one of the most dynamic, changeful coastal landscapes in England. Here is a seemingly placid place where new and profound attitudes to, and relationships with, landscape and environment are being enacted.

The forces of nature are real enough: the River Trent, which drains much of central England, meets the Ouse here, discharging huge volumes of water and sediment that flow powerfully, and dangerously for navigators, into the Humber. But the forces of mankind are no less powerful, for much of what we see is artificial, even extensively engineered, the navigation channels and also the fields reclaimed over centuries from the waters by warping – letting silt laden waters flood and settle.

The land has been built up, and now it is being let go, as bank defences have been breached at Alkborough Flats in a major scheme of flood control and natural habitat creation. Climate-change models suggest that high-tide levels are expected to increase in the Humber Estuary, in turn increasing the risk of flooding for people who live in the area. These predictions led to the decision to realign the Alkborough Flats, cutting through the flood defences to deliberately flood a site of 440 hectares (about 1,100 acres) of agricultural land on the south bank of the Humber Estuary. Opened in 2006, it is one of Europe's largest flood-storage schemes. Today the Alkborough Flats site is managed to encourage biodiversity and the development of a variety of different habitats, including intertidal mudflats and fresh and salt-water reed beds as well as wet and dry grassland.

Wilding here has replaced warping as a planned process, although the replacement is perhaps never permanent, for in this classic 'ness', of naturally shifting promontory built up by waterborne material, land will again emerge. Here is a fluent, amphibious estuarine environment far from the movements of most people to the coast, a waterland,

Left | View of a wet grassland area near Blakeney on the north Norfolk coast. Blakeney was once an important centre for European trade.

a liquid landscape, terra infirma, off the beaten tracks of tourists and artists. It is now revealed as a complex cultural and physical world in works by visual artist Simon Read and performance artist Mike Pearson, who address the difficulties of describing and depicting this place, its wider worlds and local particularities.

This is a place Mike Pearson knows well, being part of the north Lincolnshire region where he was brought up and to which he has returned in his work. The process of building up and letting go is addressed in his sound and visual work *Warplands*. The text draws on writings and images made over three centuries – history, poetry, reporting, maps and photographs – to reveal many makings and meanings of this landscape, and the many claims made upon it, from farmers to speculators, naturalists to commoners.

Warplands is in two movements, created around the idea of prospect. One is located at the turf maze in Alkbrough, looking down from the limestone escarpment. The other is down near the shore, on the flatlands, looking out from a place created by warping, close to Ousefleet. Famously the most featureless place in Britain, at least on the map, this is the emptiest kilometre square of the entire grid of the OS 1:50,000 map, crossed only in one corner by an electricity line. Each movement follows the concentric circles of the turf maze.

Left | Looking out from the turf maze at Alkborough across the flatlands of Lincolnshire. Photograph by Mike Pearson.

Sixth circle: feeling disorientated, in danger of losing track, or of drowning...
Between Trent-fall and Whitten-ness
Many are made widows and fatherless.
Goes the saying...
Trent Falls: *a perpetual rendezvous of waters;* draining one fifth of England...

Daniel Defoe looks out, in 1726:

A wonderful conflux of great rivers, all pouring down into the Humber, which
receiving the Aire, the Ouse, the Don and the Trent, becomes rather a sea than
a river.

As does parish poet Edith Spilman Dudley in 1946:

Where Humber, Ouse, and silvery Trent
Join hands at watersmeet;
Where brown-sailed barges homeward glide
On tides that never cease –

And again in 1953:

From Gunnes side o'er broadening Trent
The lovely scene which pleases much,
Tho' Lincolnshire it surely is.
Seems most peculiarly Dutch –

Visual artist Simon Read approaches this environment from a different place and perspective. His home and studio base is a sea-going barge moored on the Deben Estuary, in Suffolk, from where he has immersed himself in the dynamics of estuarine and coastal systems as he navigates the vessel around the shifting shores of eastern England. He has explored future scenarios based on forecasting and management plans on large watercolour map-works, as a way of displaying complex data from

Below | Simon Read, *The Humber Estuary from South Ferriby to Burton Stather*, 2012, watercolour on paper, using tea, coffee, tobacco, woad and indigo. Scale 1:8333.33.

various sources, of visualising and bringing otherwise submerged information to the surface. In this way, he seeks to communicate such scenes to a wider public and engage them in the conversational process of imagining environmental change. So the map-works open a space for multiple viewpoints, for the meeting of worlds, not just of land and water but also of the various communities that have a stake in them. By using watercolour on paper, he emphasises that all watery environments share the values of flow, permeability, porosity, liminality – the behaviour of the watercolour medium is itself an active part of the contemplative process, the water qualities of reflection and action.

The Humber Estuary from South Ferriby to Burton Stather is a large artwork in the tradition of a display map, which explores the wider context of the Alkborough Flats Tidal Defence Scheme, and makes connection with Mike Pearson's *Warplands*. The areal scope of map-work is comparable; and the turf labyrinth, Julian's Bower, forms a component of the work by placing it as a base layer of the drawing.

When commissioned to make the work, Read started from a position of being ignorant of the site itself but aware of the range of processes to which it would be subjected. As a consequence he decided that he would explore the conditions that drove the decision to realign the Alkborough Flats by mapping the wider context, encompassing the Humber Estuary, the confluence of the Trent and Ouse at Trent Falls and the topography of those areas immediately adjacent to the site both to the north and south of the estuary. Since this exercise is more disinterested than the projects carried out on the Suffolk Coast where he has a specific community role, he felt free to explore further the integrity of the drawing process in relation to the enquiry.

The work makes clear the dilemma of Flood Risk Management in an estuarine environment that is populous, highly industrialised and agriculturally extremely productive. The estuary is shown to be predominantly flood-dominant. This is clear from the sandbanks within the main estuary, where the sand drops out first from the flood but is sculpted by the ebb into long tails. The saltings, mudflats and sandbanks are negotiable territories, their identity is fluid and porous. As a drawing, they can be perceived as continuous to the sea on the flood or a part of the land on the ebb. The making of the drawing reflects the relationship with natural processes that is characteristic of the development of a workable shoreline management plan. Control and acquiescence must be equal partners, just as in a drawing or painting the behaviour of a medium and the process itself is key to the degree that either may be manipulated.

Above | A view of the intertidal zone on the north edge of Morston Marsh at Blakeney Point, Norfolk.

Shelter from the Storm

The South West peninsula, of Cornwall, Devon and Somerset, is, as the atlas shows, a highly concentrated coastal region, with more than 435 miles of coastline in the intricate pattern of rocky headlands and beaches that has long made the southwest a magnet for tourists. The South West Coast path (the UK's longest national trail) originated as a route for the Coastguard to walk from lighthouse to lighthouse patrolling for smugglers, looking down into every bay and cove.

Walking the path in south Cornwall, along the Lizard Peninsula, we look down into one of the most picturesque spots, Mullion Cove. From a height it seems a perfect specimen: cobbled slipways, with nets and lobster pots, run down to a stone harbour, an image of timeless tranquillity that perhaps pulls at deeper emotional bonds to secure havens, offering shelter from storms of all kinds. A closer look is more unsettling, however. The National Trust plaque declares that since 1990 more than £500,000 has been spent on repairs and maintenance of the harbour – and that figure has now doubled. The harbour walls show the patchy evidence of such work, including some cracks that are opening up.

The fact is, the structure is being undermined by increasingly powerful storm surges and is proving unaffordable to maintain. The current National Trust policy of 'working with the grain of nature' means that eventually, perhaps sooner rather than later, this much-loved landmark will be left to disintegrate, rather challenging the Trust's motto 'forever for everyone'. Mullion Harbour is a test case not only for coastal sites at risk

Above | Mullion Cove is a popular place for coasteering. An organised group leaps off the harbour wall one by one in preparation for scrambling and jumping from rocks.

Left | View of boats sheltering behind the harbour wall at Mullion Cove, the Lizard, Cornwall.

in the South West but for shorelines more widely, even all landscapes. How might such a future scenario for Mullion Cove be presented to an unsuspecting public?

Cultural geographer Caitlin de Silvey has suggested that a way forward is to present this future as part of a longer, dynamic, discontinuous history in the past, within a narrative that anticipates decline and destruction. The harbour is historically recent, built in 1895, as part of a large-scale venture to fish for pilchards in the face of declining catches. The venture failed and a structure that was expensive to build became even more costly as constant repairs were needed against winter storms. Constructed on a geological fault line, the harbour should probably not have been built there in the first place. It is a kind of folly, albeit one that has became a key part of the tourist scenery of the place.

Shortly after the harbour was built, the Great Western Railway built a large hotel on the cliff above. As it turned out, the railway never came directly to Mullion, but sufficient numbers of tourists made it there by road. The National Trust played a key role in sustaining tourism by accepting the gift of the harbour in October 1945, despite years of deferred maintenance having taken their toll. Visitor numbers rose, particularly from the 1960s with the great rise in car ownership, when Mullion Harbour featured on the cover of the Batsford Guide to Devon and Cornwall. At the same time this provoked a familiar, misguided, complaint, echoed by Ronald Duncan, the author of the Batsford Guide:

Above | Photograph of Mullion Cove, taken c.1890, before the harbour wall was built. Fishing boats have been dragged up the beach beyond the reach of the high tide.

I knew it when I was a child before so much of this coast had been turned into a car park. I can remember the fishing villages when the fisherman were fisherman. The Council for the Preservation of Rural England and the National Trust are supposed to do something to preserve our inheritance. It is obviously too late to prevent the desecration that has occurred. Clearly unless the whole of the Cornish coast is to be raided by vandals, some new legislation is required.

A more realistic narrative, particularly now, would be to address the predicaments of preservation and process, to acknowledge the long- and short-term cycles of development and disintegration, of the making and unmaking of the landscape, its mobility as well as its stability, fluidity as well as fixity. Like other plans and projections for landscape, this is a form of 'anticipatory history'. Despite its tranquil, timeless appearance on a summer's day, Mullion has been marked, seasonally and historically, by both routine and extreme episodes of change and transformation. The prospect is a policy of managed retreat, which will see only limited maintenance of the breakwaters carried out, allowing ruin, but not dereliction.

Like the proverbial owner of a scenic folly, the Trust will keep this ruin in good repair but may need to go beyond picturesque aesthetics, to a more sublime presentation of deep time, destructive storms and human frailty. It may even need to envisage a reversion to a more naturalistic state of landscape. Mullion Harbour might become again Mullion Cove, open to the sea, boats beached on the shingle – as it was pictured in postcards before the construction of the harbour walls. To understand the past accurately may help to manage the future effectively. In landscape, as in life, we may need to learn to let go. But it is a hard lesson, and any long-term stories we might want to tell about unstable landscapes like Mullion Harbour can be overtaken by events. These include the succession of sea surges that ravaged the South West of England in the winter of 2013, which prompted action to shore up all kinds of built structures along the coast, and reactivated a more security-conscious story of landscape development.

A Changing Coastline

Coastlines are by their nature highly dynamic. Rising sea levels and the increased incidence of extreme weather events makes them even more so. Shifting shorelines make the work of conservation on the coast even more important, yet also pose difficult questions about how much we are prepared to lose in order to adapt to changing conditions. Erosion of land into the sea can be a highly emotive topic on the coast, with profound implications for people's livelihoods and wellbeing. Adaptation to new conditions remains essential, however, if we are to mitigate the worst excesses of climate change.

Left | Northey Island is a tidal island located in the Blackwater Estuary just off the coast of Essex. The island plays an important role in the dynamics of the estuary, helping to dissipate the pressure of high tides before they reach the town of Maldon. Northey was one of the very first places in the UK where adaptation approaches were tested, when farmland here was allowed to be inundated with saltwater in order to extend the area of saltmarsh.

Left | View to the Mourne Mountains from Murlough National Nature Reserve, County Down. The nature reserve is a fragile 6,000-year-old sand dune system. The dune fields were badly affected during the winter storms of 2013/2014, but conservation has focused on allowing the system to be mobile, so that dunes can start to form elsewhere along this stretch of coast.

Right | View of the storm-damaged cliffs and beach at Birling Gap, East Sussex, pictured in February 2014, with demolition work taking place on vulnerable cliff-top buildings. Extreme weather in January and February of that year resulted in seven years' worth of erosion at Birling Gap in just a few weeks. As a consequence, the National Trust was forced to demolish buildings at risk of collapse.

Left | Kayaking and windsurfing around Thurlestone Rock off South Milton Sands, Devon. The winter storms of 2013/2014 caused significant damage to the dunes at South Milton Sands, and substantial repairs were needed including a new boardwalk.

Below | Formby Point, Liverpool, has the largest area of dunes anywhere in the country. However, the dunes face constant erosion, despite past attempts to stabilise them by encouraging the growth of marram grass. Today, a modern response is to invite donations of Christmas trees, which provide stability for the dunes and allow the sand and grass to build up.

Above | View of the storm-damaged cliffs and beach on the south shore of Brownsea Island, Dorset, pictured in February 2014. The extreme weather resulted in cliff falls and rapid erosion of the coastline. The National Trust is working with natural processes and removing failing sea defences from the 1970s to restore some of the coastline.

Right | Studland Beach in Dorset stretches for 4 miles to the chalk cliffs of Handfast Point and Old Harry Rocks, including Shell Bay. Behind it is a heathland, which has national nature reserve status, and a long row of beach huts. One of the initiatives following the severe storms of 2013/2014 is to design a 'future proof' beach hut that can withstand extreme weather.

Acknowledgements

Many of the projects which inspired this book were funded through the Arts and Humanities Research Council's Landscape and Environment programme.

Gail Lambourne, formerly the Programme Manager at AHRC and Charlotte Lloyd, formerly Programme Co-ordinator at Nottingham, proved strongly supportive colleagues, as well as great company. The book is dedicated to them.

Some programme projects inform the book directly through their subject matter, as case studies of places; others shape it more through their perspective.

We are particularly grateful to the following project researchers: Nicholas Alfrey, Martin Allen, Caroline Anderson, Polly Atkin, Graeme Barker, Stephen Bottoms, Nick Branch, Sally Bushell, Andrew Church, Peter Coates, Sarah Cohen, Matthew Cragoe, Caitlin de Silvey, Marianna Dudley, Christopher Dyer, Mark Hallett, Matthew Flintham, Matthew Gandy, Stephanie Jones, Caroline Juby, Patrick Keiller, Hayden Lorimer, Doreen Massey, Briony McDonagh, Mike Pearson, Geoff Quilley, Simon Read, Christine Riding, Chris Rodgers, Dan Shipsides, Andrew Spicer, Divya Tolia-Kelley, Ian Waites, Charles Withers, Rob Witcher and Patrick Wright.

We also wish to thank members of the programme Directorate and Advisory Board including Aoife Duggan, Lowri Jones, John Rink, David Austin, Ann Boddington, Nigel Llewellyn, Graham Fairclough, Paul Holm, Edward Impey, Sally Mackey, Martin Postle and Catherine Souch.

We acknowledge the support of the following programme partners: English Heritage, Landscape Research Group, Le:Notre, Royal Geographical Society and Tate.

We have also benefitted from the advice of colleagues at the University of Nottingham, including Oliver Dunnett, Georgina Endfield, David Matless, Julie Sanders, Susanne Seymour and Charles Watkins.

We are grateful to John Stachiewicz (now of Tate) for supporting the inception of this project during his time at the National Trust and to Katie Bond for her support and encouragement as the National Trust's publisher. A number of National Trust properties collaborated with the Landscape and Environment programme, and our thanks go to all of these. In particular we enjoyed working with Keith Zealand and Malcolm Fisher at Sheringham in Norfolk, who were very willing to share their time and expertise in order to promote the objectives of the programme.

Selected Bibliography

Introduction: Revealing Landscapes
www.landscape.ac.uk
Hoskins, W.G. *The Making of the English Landscape*, London 1976
Matless, David *Landscape and Englishness*, Reaktion 1998
Roberts, Simon *We English*, Chris Boot 2009

Chapter 1: The Art of Landscape
Coates, Peter *A Story of Six Rivers: History, Culture and Ecology*, Reaktion 2013
Daniels, Stephen *Fields of Vision: Landscape Imagery and National Identity in England and the United States*, Polity 1992
Drabble, Margaret *A Writer's Britain*, Thames and Hudson 2009
Doran, Susan (ed.) *Royal River: Power, Pageantry and the Thames*, Scala 2012
Dimbleby, David (ed.) *A Picture of Britain*, Tate Publishing 2005
Quilley, Geoff and Bonehill, John *William Hodges: The Art of Exploration*, Yale University Press 2004
Keiller, Patrick *Robinson in Space*, Reaktion 1999
Leonard, M. and Strachan, R. *The Beat Goes On: Liverpool, Popular Music and the Changing City*, Liverpool University Press 2009
Rosenthal, Michael *Constable: A Painter and His Landscape*, Yale University Press 1982
Tufnell, Ben *Land Art*, Tate Publishing 2006

Chapter 2: Ancient Places
Hingley, Richard *Hadrian's Wall: A Life*, Oxford University Press 2012
Keiller, Patrick *The Possibility of Life's Survival on the Planet*, Tate Publishing 2012
Pearson, Mike Parker *Stonehenge: Exploring the Greatest Stone Age Mystery*, Simon & Schuster 2012
Pearson, Mike *'In Comes I': Performance, Memory and Landscape*, University of Exeter Press 2007
Samuel, Raphael *Island Stories*, Verso Books 1998
Smiles, Sam *The Image of Antiquity: Ancient Britain and the Romantic Imagination*, Yale University Press 1994
Spicer, Andrew (ed.) *The Parish Church in the Early Modern World*, Ashgate 2015
Walsham, Alexandra *The Reformation of the Landscape*, Oxford University Press 2011

Chapter 3: Homes and Gardens
Alfrey, Nicholas, Daniels, Stephen and Postle, Martin (eds) *Art of the Garden*, Tate Publishing 2004
Daniels, Stephen *Humphry Repton: Landscape Gardening and the Geography of Georgian England*, Yale University Press 1999
Daniels, Stephen and Veale, Lucy *Humphry Repton at Sheringham Park: Bringing Landscape to Life*, 1812-2012, University of Nottingham 2010
Driver, Felix *Power and Pauperism, The Workhouse System, 1834-1884*, Cambridge University Press, 2004
Evans, Sian *Life Below Stairs: In the Victorian & Edwardian Country House*, National Trust 2011
Greaves, Lydia *Houses of the National Trust*, National Trust, 2013
Lacey, Stephen *Gardens of the National Trust*, National Trust, 2011
Robinson, J. M. *Felling the Ancient Oaks: How England Lost its Great Country Estates*, Aurum Press Ltd, 2012

Strong, Roy, Binney, Marcus and Harris, John *The Destruction of the Country House*, Thames and Hudson 1974
Wright, Patrick *The Village that Died for England*, Faber and Faber 2002

Chapter 4: Lost in the Woods
Cowell, Ben *Sir Robert Hunter*, Pitkin 2013
Deakin, Roger *Wildwood: A Journey Through Trees*, Hamish Hamilton 2007
Linebaugh, Peter *The Magna Carta Manifesto*, University of California 2006
Maitland, Sarah *Gossip from the Forest: The Tangled Roots of Our Forests and Fairytales*, Granta 2013
Murphy, Graham *The Founders of the National Trust*, National Trust 2002
Rackham, Oliver *Woodlands*, Collins 2006
Rackham, Oliver *The Last Forest: The Story of Hatfield Forest*, J.M. Dent & Sons 1989
Schama, Simon *Landscape and Memory*, Harper Collins 1995
Watkins, Charles *Trees, Woods and Forests: A Social and Cultural History*, Reaktion 2014

Chapter 5: Open Country
Cragoe, Matthew and Readman, Paul (eds) *The Land Question in Britain 1750-1950*, Palgrave 2010
Darley, Gillian *Octavia Hill*, Francis Boutle 2010
Jenkins, Simon *England's 100 Best Views*, Profile 2013
Macfarlane, Robert *The Old Ways*, Penguin 2013
Neeson, J. M. *Commoners: Common Right, Enclosure and Social Change in England, 1700-1820*, Cambridge University Press 1993
Rodgers, C. P., Straughton, E. A., Winchester, A. J. L., and Pieraccini, M. *Contested Common Land: Environmental Governance Past and Present*, Earthscan 2010
Thomas, Keith *Man and the Natural World*, Oxford University Press 1983
Walton, J. K., and Wood, J. *The Making of a Cultural Landscape: The English Lake District as a Tourist Destination, 1750-2010*, Ashgate 2013
Waites, Ian *Common Land in English Painting 1700-1850*, Boydell 2012

Chapter 6: Shifting Shores
DeSilvey, Caitlin, Naylor, Simon, and Sackett, Colin (Eds) *Anticipatory History*, Uniformbooks 2011
Gogerty, Clare *The National Trust Book of the Coast*, National Trust 2015
Payne, Christiana *Where the Sea Meets the Land: Artists on the Coast in Nineteenth Century Britain*, Sansom 2007
Pearson, Chris, Coates, Peter, and Cole, Tim (Eds) *Militarised Landscapes: From Gettysburg to Salisbury Plain*, Continuum 2010
Pye-Smith, Charlie *In Search of Neptune: A Celebration of the National Trust's Coastline*, National Trust 1990
Riding, Christine and Johns, Richard *Turner and the Sea*, Thames and Hudson 2014
Sebald, W. G. *The Rings of Saturn*, 1995, translated into English by Michael Hulse, Vintage Classics 2002
Shifting shores in the South-West, living with a changing coastline, National Trust 2008
Symmons Roberts, Michael, and Farley, Paul *Edgelands: Journeys into England's True Wilderness*, Vintage 2012

Credits

Index

Figures in italics indicate captions.

Abbot Hall Art Gallery, Kendal, Cumbria 27
Abraham Brothers: 'Climbers on Napes Needle' 27
Acland, Sir Thomas 197
Acorn Bank, Cumbria 167
Adam, Robert 109
Adey, John 135
Air Force, Cumbria 169
Aire River 287
Aislabie, John 125
Aislabie, William 125
Aldermaston, AWE, Berkshire 283
Alkborough Flats, Lincolnshire 285–286, 289
Alkborough Flats Tidal Defence Scheme 289
Alkborough, Lincolnshire 97–99, 98
see also Julian's Bower
Allan Bank, Grasmere, Cumbria 28, 29, 29
Ancholme River 39
Anglesey Abbey, Cambridgeshire 48, 50
Ship Bedroom 49
Ankerwycke Yew, Priory Wood, opposite Runnymede 180, 180, 181, 181
Antarctica 50
Antony, Cornwall 193
Arlington Court, Devon 198
Arnold, Matthew: 'Dover Beach' 256
Arts Council England 58
Arts and Humanities Research Council: Landscape and Environment programme 10
Ashness Farm, Lake District, Cumbria 12
Ashridge Estate, Hertfordshire 167, 192
Frithsden beeches 176
Atomic Weapons Research Establishment (AWRE) 279, 283
Avebury, Wiltshire 68, 69
Avon River 73, 104

Badbury Rings, Dorset 81
Bankes family 95
Barafundle Bay, Pembrokeshire, Wales 263
Barmouth Beach, Gwynedd 259
Barry, Charels 67
Bateman, James 143, 199
Batsford, Harry: How to See the Country 214
Beatles, the 54, 54, 153, 155
Beaulieu Abbey, Hampshire 226
Becher, Rev. J.T. 141
Bedingfeld, Sir Edmund 125
Bedruthan Steps beach, Cornwall 59
Benson, A.C. 43
Benson, E.F. 43
Mapp and Lucia series 43
Berkhamsted Common, Hertfordshire 214
Bexhill-on-Sea, East Sussex 275
Biddulph Grange, Staffordshire 143
Pinetum 201
The Stumpery 192
Wellingtonia Avenue 199
Bird How, Eskdale, Cumbria 241
Birling Gap, East Sussex 60, 256, 295
Birmingham 113
50-54 Inge Street and 55-64 Hurst Street 120, 121
Black Down properties, National Trust 185
Blackwater Estuary, Essex 277, 295
Blaise Hamlet, Gloucestershire 118, 119, 121
Blakeney, Norfolk 267, 285

Blakeney Point, Norfolk 255, 289
Blenheim Palace, Woodstock, Oxfordshire 117
Blickling Estate, Norfolk 227, 250
Blickling Hall, Norfolk 123
Bodley, G.F. 108
Bodnant Garden, Conwy, Wales 144
Pin Mill, Canal Terrace 144
Boleyn, Ann 180
Bollin River 123
Borrowdale, near Grange, Cumbria 8
Borrowdale Yews, Lake District 179, 180
Bosherton Lakes, Pembrokeshire, Wales 263
Bossington, Somerset 286
Bossington Beach, Holnicote Estate, Somerset 259
Bournville, Birmingham 121
Brancaster, Norfolk 244
Brancaster Millennium Activity Centre 246
Brancaster Staithe, Norfolk 244
Brandelhow, Derwentwater, Cumbria 204
Brent River 56
Bridgeman, Charles 124
Bridport Sands, Burton Cliff, Dorset 275
Brighton, Sussex 129
Brimham Rocks, Nidderdale, North Yorkshire 33
Bristol 75
Bristol, Frederick Hervey, 9th Earl of (the Earl Bishop) 33
Bristol High Cross 65, 65
British Society of Foresters 204
Brown, Lancelot 'Capability' 92, 95, 109, 127, 129
Brownsea Island, Dorset 297
Burges, William 99

Cadgwith, the Lizard, Cornwall 249
Calais, France 275
Calke Abbey, Derbyshire 114
Cambridge 249
Canaletto 55
Carisle 84
carrlands 39, 40
Carta de Foresta (Charter of the Forest) 181, 183
Castle Crag, Cumbria 8
Castlerigg Stone Circle, near Keswick, Cumbria 65
Cerne Abbas Giant, Dorset 76, 76, 77
Chalfont St Giles, Buckinghamshire 29
Chartists 157
Chartres Cathedral, France 99
Chichester Canal 129
Chilterns 194
Christie, Agatha: Dead Man's Folly 161
Churches Conservation Trust 109
Churchill, Sir Winston 213
Clare, John: Remembrances 233
Claremont Landscape Garden, Surrey 124
Clayton, John 85
Clayton Wall, Hadrian's Wall 85
Cliveden, Buckinghamshire 57, 57
Cliveden Set 57
Clumber Park, Nottinghamshire 108, 117, 117, 118, 149, 225
Coates, Peter: A Story of Six Rivers 54
Coggeshall, Essex 226
Coleridge, Samuel Taylor 21, 25, 26, 28, 31
Colt Hoare, Richard 73
Commons Preservation Society 187, 188, 234, 244, 246
Commons Registration Act (1965) 239, 244

Coniston Fells, Cumbria 22
Coniston Water, Cumbria 22
Constable, John 9, 35–37, 39, 42, 55, 233
Branch Hill Pond, Hampstead Head, with a Boy Sitting on a Bank 234
Flatford Mill ('Scene on a Navigable River') 34
Hampstead Heath paintings 233–234
The Hay Wain 35
The Mill Stream 35
The Opening of Waterloo Bridge (Whitehall Stairs, June 18th, 1817) 55, 56
The White Horse 35
Willy Lott's House on the River Stour, Suffolk 35
Constable Country 29, 35, 36, 37, 39
Conwy River 249
Cook, Captain James 49, 50, 50
Copt Hall Marshes, Essex 277
Corfe Castle, Dorset 95
Cornish Mining World Heritage Site 265
Cornwall 267, 290
Corporation of the City of London 187
Cotehele estate, near Saltash, Cornwall 4
Cotman, John Sell: A View of Mousehold Heath from Silver Road 229
Cotswolds 20
Council for the Preservation of Rural England 293
Country Houses Scheme 123, 156
Cragside, Northumberland 207, 207
Crayford, Kent 139
Croft Castle, Herefordshire 179, 179
'Tell it to the Trees' exhibition (2009-10) 59
Cromer, Norfolk 267, 268
Cromwell, Oliver 76, 109
Croome Park, Croome d'Abitot, Worcestershire: St Mary Magdalene church 109
Crowdundle Beck 167
Cumbria 35
Cunard Cowboys 53

Danbury Common, Essex 188
Dart River 161
Darwin, Charles 47
de Quincey, Thomas 28
de Silvery, Caitlin 291
Debdon Burn 207
Deben Estuary, Suffolk 81, 288
Defoe, Daniel 48, 287
Derby 192
Derwent Moors, Peak District 65
Derwent River 8
Derwentwater, Cumbria 19, 22
Devil's Dyke, South Downs, West Sussex 214
Devil's Punch Bowl, Hindhead Commons, Surrey 9, 246–247, 247
Devon 31, 263, 290
Dickens, Charles 270
Dieppe, France 275
Dinas Oleu, Barmouth, Gwynedd 256, 259, 260
Dinefwr Park, Llandeilo, Carmarthenshire 168
Dobson, John 85
Dockens Water, New Forest, Hampshire 171
Dolaucothi Gold Mines, Llanwrda, Carmarthenshire 79
Dolmelynllyn Estate, Gwynedd 237
Don River 287
Donati's Comet 272
Dorset 31, 75, 77
Dove Cottage, Grasmere, Cumbria 27, 28, 29

Dove River 236
Dovedale, Derbyshire 236
Dragon Hill, Oxfordshire 75
Druids 73
Duddon Valley, Lake District 239
Dudley, Edith Spilman 287
Duffy, Carol Ann: 'White Cliffs' 255, 256
Duncan, Ronald 291, 293
Devon & Cornwall (Batsford Guide) 291
Dunham Massey, Cheshire 123
Dunstanburgh Castle, Northumberland 85, 93
Dunwich Heath and Beach, Suffolk 261
Durham University 83
Durrington Walls, North-West Somerset 73
Dyce, William: Pegwell Bay - A Recollection of October 5th 1858 271–272, 272, 275

Eames, Charles and Ray 159
Easterby, Caitlin 60
Edale Valley, Peak District 65
Egremont, Earls of 127, 129
3rd Earl of 129
Eight Wantz Ways, Hatfield Forest, Essex 168
Eley, Henry: Geology in the Garden or, The Fossils in the Flint Pebbles 271
Elliot, Dave 185
Emin, Tracey 275
Enclosure Acts 216
English Channel 213, 264, 275
English Heritage 84, 99
Ennerdale, Cumbria 207
Ennerdale Valley, Lake District National Park, Cumbria 250
Epping Forest 187, 188, 188, 244
Epstein, Brian 153
Ermine Street 98
Esk River 241
'Esk Twenty-Four Book' 241, 243
Eskdale, Cumbria 25, 241, 243, 244
Eskdale Common, Cumbria 237, 239
Eskdale Commoners Association 239, 241
Essex 35, 277
European Landscape Convention (2000) 8
Exmoor Singers 283

Fairhaven, 1st Lord 48
Fell & Rock Climbing Club 27
Felbrigg Estate, Norfolk: St Margaret's church 250
Figsbury Ring, Wiltshire 67
Flagstonehenge, Dorset 75
Flatford Mill, East Bergholt, Suffolk 15, 34, 36, 36, 37, 37, 39, 42
Fleming, Ian 157
Flintham, Matthew 280
Florence, Linda 61
Folkestone, Kent 275
Forest of Arden, Warwickshire 171, 174
Forest of Dean, Gloucestershire 174, 204, 209
Forestry Commission 177, 203–204, 203, 205, 207, 207, 209
Formby Point, Merseyside 80, 296
Forthlin Road (no.20), Allerton, Liverpool 150, 152–153, 153, 154, 155, 155
Foulness, Essex 279
Fountains Abbey, North Yorkshire 101, 102, 103–104, 165
Fox, Wilfrid 194, 195
Fox Talbot, William Henry 45, 104
Friar's Crag, Derwentwater, Cumbria 22
Frontiers of the Roman Empire World Heritage Site 89

Gadder River *125*
Gainsborough, Thomas 185
　Cornard Wood, near Sudbury, Suffolk 175
Galloway Forest Park, Argyllshire *203*
Garibaldi, Giuseppe 89
Gathering/Yr Helfa, The (walking
　performance) *59*
Giant's Causeway, County Antrim *31, 33*
Gibbons, Grinling 129
Gibbs, James *93*
Gibside, Newcastle-upon-Tyne
　Orangery *93*
　Palladian Chapel *107*
Gilbert and George 148–149
Gilpin, Sawrey *171*
Gimson, Ernest *157*
Gimson, Sidney *157*
Gimson family *157*
Glandford, Norfolk *97*
Glastonbury Tor, Somerset 75–76, *75,*
　102
Gloucestershire 54
Godolphin House, near Helston,
　Cornwall: Cider House *225*
Golden Cap, Dorset *31*
Goldfinger, Ernö *157*
Goulton, Thomas 99
Goulton-Constable, John 99
Grainger, Percy 40–41
Grasmere, Cumbria 28, *28*
Great Coxwell Barn, near Faringdon,
　Oxfordshire *226*
Great Gable, Cumbria 27, *27*
Great Gale (1987) *177, 177*
Great Langdale, Lake District *19, 21*
Great Mewstone, Plymouth, Devon *263*
Great Western Railway 291
Greater Manchester *123*
Greenham Common, Berkshire 56
Greenway, Devon *161*
Gunness, North Lincolnshire 287
Gwynne, Patrick *113, 159*

Hadrian's Wall 11, 83–86, *83, 84, 85,* 89,
　91, 205
Hadrian's Wall Path, near Steel Rigg,
　Henshaw, Northumberland *299*
Hafod Y Llan Farm, Snowdonia *59*
　Watkin Path *238*
Hainault, London 187
Hamburg, Germany 53, 54
Hampstead Heath Act (1871) 234
Handfast Point, Dorset *297*
Hardknott Pass, Lake District 239
Hardman, Edward Chambré *161*
Hardman, Margaret *161*
Hardwicke, Philip Yorke, 1st Earl of *95*
Hardy, Thomas *43,* 73, 75
　Jude the Obscure 43
　Tess of the d'Urbervilles 43, 75
Hare Street, Romford, Essex 147
Harling Down, West Sussex *61*
Harrison, George *150*
Harrison Stickle, Lake District *19*
Haslemere, Surrey 186
Hatfield Forest, Essex *165, 168, 173, 177*
Hawkes, Jacquetta 71
Henrhyd Falls, Brecon Beacons, Powys *33*
Henry VIII, King 180
Heritage Lottery Fund 58
Hertfordshire *167*
Heysham Head, Lancashire: St Patrick's
　Chapel *107*
Hibaldstow, Lincolnshire 99
Hidcote, Gloucestershire: Mrs Winthrop's
　Garden *144*
High Peak Moors, Peak District National
　Park *251*
Highlands of Scotland 21
Hill, Octavia 246
Hill Top, Sawrey, near Ambleside,
　Cumbria *47*

Himalayas 192
Hindhead Common, Surrey Hills *174*
Hingley, Richard 83
Hoare, Henry *107*
Hoare, Henry, II ('the Magnificent') *123*
Hod Hill, Dorset *79*
Hodges, William
　Jacques and the Wounded Stag: 'As You
　　Like It', Act II, Scene 1 171
　View of Oaitepeha Bay, Tahiti 49, 50, *50*
Homewood, The, Surrey *113, 159*
Horkstow, North Lincolnshire 40–41
Horkstow Bridge, Horkstow Carrs, North
　Lincolnshire 40, *41*
Hoskins, W.G.: *The Making of the English*
　Landscape 280
Hotbank Crags, Northumberland 85, *86*
Household Words magazine 270
Housesteads Fort, Hadrian's Wall 84, *84,*
　85, *91*
Howard, Ebenezer 113
Howard, Luke 234
Humber Estuary 39, 97, 98, *98,* 285,
　287, 289
Hunter Basecamp, Swan Barn Farm,
　Surrey *185*
Hunter, Robert 186–187, *188,* 246
Hutchinson, Sara 25
Hutton, James 270

Ibsley Common, New Forest, Hampshire
　217
Ightham Mote, Kent *124*
Isle of Wight 216

James, Henry *43*
Jerusalem 99
John, King 182, 183
"John Bull" 264, *264*
John of Gaunt *93*
John the Baptist 97
Johnes family *79*
Johnston, Major Lawrence *144*
Jones, Stephanie 48
Joseph of Arimathea 102
Julian's Bower, Alkborough, Lincolnshire
　98–99, *98,* 286, *287,* 289
　see also Alkborough
Julius, son of Aeneas of Troy 98
Jupiter Point, Cornwall *193*
Jurassic Coast *31,* 118, 275, *275*
Jurassic Park (film) 275

Keiller, Patrick 56, *56,* 68, 69
Kent 114
Kielder Forest Park, Northumberland
　205, *205, 207, 209*
Kielder Water 15, *205,* 207
Killerton, Devon *197*
Kinder Scout, Peak District 65
　Zig Zag climbing route *26, 27*
Kingston Lacy, Dorset *199*
Kingston Lacy Estate, Dorset *79, 95*
Kirk Fell, Cumbria *241*

Lacock Abbey, Wiltshire *45, 103,* 104,
　104, 105, 119
Lacock village, near Chippenham *10,*
　119, 121
Lake District 12, 15, 19, 21, 22, *22, 25,*
　27, 42, *47,* 203, *239, 243*
Lamb House, Rye, East Sussex *43*
Langdyke Bush, Helpston Heath 231, *233*
Langham Pond, Runnymede meadow,
　Old Windsor, Surrey *182*
Law, Ben: *The Woodland Way* 185
Lawrence, D.H. 149
Lawrence, Philippa: *Bound 59*
Leconfield, Lords 239
Leith Hill Place, Dorking, Surrey *47, 191*
Lennon, John 54, 150, *150,* 151, 152, *152,*
　153, *154,* 155

LIFE projects *249*
Lincoln 98
Lincolnshire 39, 40, 285, 286, 287
Lingmell Gill, Cumbria *25*
Lingwood Common, Essex *188*
Liverpool 53–54
　59 Rodney Street *161*
　'The Beat Goes On' exhibition (2008)
　　54
　Beatles Story exhibition, Albert Dock *54*
　Cavern Club 54
　Museum of Liverpool *53*
Liverpool University: Institute of Popular
　Music 54
Lizard Peninsula 290
Lobb, William *197*
London 54–57, 68
　Balfron Tower, Poplar *157*
　Bank of England *227*
　Brent Cross 56
　Brentford 56
　Finsbury Health Centre 213
　Hampstead: 2 Willow Road *157*
　Hampstead Heath 233–234, *234,* 244
　Millbank Penitentiary 141
　Palace of Westminster 67
　South Bank 56
　Whitehall Stairs 56
London (film) 56
Londonderry, Edith, Lady *145*
Long, Richard: *Cerne Abbas Walk* 75, 76,
　77
Lopping Hall, Loughton, Essex *188*
Lothian, Philip Kerr, Lord *123*
Ludshott Common, East Hampshire *233*
Lulworth firing range, Dorset 118
Lutyens, Marcos and Marianantoni,
　Alessandro: *CO²morrow* art project *118*
Lyd River *169*
Lydford Gorge, Devon *169*
Lyell, Charles 272
　Principles of Geology 270
Lynher River *193*
Lynn, Dame Vera *33,* 255, 256

McCartney, Jim 153
McCartney, Mary 153
McCartney, Mike 153, *155*
McCartney, Paul 54, 150–153, *150, 152,*
　153, 154, 155
Macfarlane, Robert: *The Old Ways* 80
Magna Carta 180, 181, 182, 183, 187
Maitland, Reverend John Whitaker 187
Maldon, Essex *295*
Mam Tor, Peak District 65, *80*
Manchester *251*
Manger, Oxfordshire *75*
Margate, Kent 271, 273, 275
　Turner Contemporary Gallery 275
Marianantoni, Alessandro 118
Marine and Coastal Access Act (2009)
　256
Massachusetts Trustees of Reservation
　246
Max Gate, Dorchester, Dorset *43,* 73, 75
Mendip Hills *150*
Mendips, *241* Menlove Avenue, Woolton,
　Merseyside 150–153, *150, 151, 152,*
　155
Mersey River 53, 54
Merseybeat 53, 54
Merseyside 54
Messel, Ludwig *95*
Metropolitan Board of Works 234
Midhurst, West Sussex 214
Midwich Cuckoos, The (Wyndham) 280
Migneint blanket bog, Wybrant Valley,
　Gwynedd *249*
Miller, Sanderson *95*
Milton, John 29
　Paradise Lost 22
Ministry of Defence *263*

Minsmere Reserve, Suffolk *261*
Monet, Claude 56
Monk's House, East Sussex *11, 43*
Morris, William 226
Morris Motor Car Co. 159
Morston Marsh, Blakeney Point, Norfolk
　289
Mount Grace Priory, Yorkshire Moors
　102
Mount Stewart, County Down *145*
Mountain, Sir Brian *31*
Mourne Mountains, County Down *295*
Mousehold Heath, Norwich, Norfolk *229*
Mr Straw's House: 'Endcliffe', Blythe
　Grove, Worksop, Nottinghamshire
　147–150, *147, 148, 149*
Mullion Cove, the Lizard, Cornwall 290,
　290, 291, 293
Mullion Harbour, the Lizard, Cornwall
　290–291, *293*
Murlough National Nature Reserve,
　County Down *295*

Napoleon Bonaparte 137, 264, 267
Nash, John 118, *119*
National Land Company *157*
National Trust Act (1907) 186, 246
Natural England 256
Needles, the, Isle of Wight *261*
Needles Old Battery, Isle of Wight *264*
Needles Passage, Isle of Wight *264*
Needwood Forest, Staffordshire 174
Nelson, Admiral Lord Horatio 267
Neptune Coastline Campaign 9, 256,
　260, *261*
New Forest, Hampshire 204, 209, *217,*
　230
New Forest Commoners *171*
Newbould, Frank: 'Your Britain - Fight
　For It Now' 213–214, *213*
Newcastle, Henry Pelham-Clinton, 5th
　Duke of *108*
Newcastle-upon-Tyne 84, 85
Newtimber Hall, Devil's Dyke, South
　Downs, West Sussex *251*
Newton, Sir Isaac 179–180
Nicholson, Norman 239, 241
Nicolson, Adam *45*
Nicolson, Harold *45, 225*
Norfolk 97, 130, 135, 192
North Antrim Coast *79*
North Downs *33*
North Sea 39, 54, *81, 133,* 137, 268, *279*
Northamptonshire *231*
Northey Island, Essex *277, 295*
Northumberland *93,* 267
Northumberland, Earls of 239
Northumberland National Park 84
Nuffield, Lady *159*
Nuffield Place, Oxfordshire *159*
Nuffield, William Morris, Lord *159*
Nuffield Place, Oxfordshire *159*
Nymans, West Sussex *95, 145*

O'Connor, Feargus *157*
Old Harry Rocks, Isle of Purbeck, Dorset
　275, 297
Ono, Yoko 152
Ordnance Survey *20, 21,* 75, 76
Orford Ness, Suffolk 259, 279–280, *279,*
　283
　Lighthouse 283, *283*
　Radar Tower *280*
　Stony Ditch *280*
Otmoor, Oxfordshire 221, 223
Ouse River 285, 287, 289
Ousefleet, Yorkshire 286
Oxburgh Hall, Norfolk *125*
Oxford 223
　Abingdon Road *68*
Oxfordshire 54, 57

Pacific Ocean *50*
Padley Gorge, Longshaw Estate, Derbyshire *167*
Paine, James *93*
Pascoe, Simon *60*
Pavey Ark, Lake District *19*
Peak District *26*, *65*
Pearson, Mike 40, *40*, 286, *287*
   Carrlands 40
   In Comes I 99
   Warplands 286–287, 289
Pegwell Bay, Kent *271*
Pen y Fan, Brecon Becons, Powys *31*
Pennard Pill *4*
Petworth House and Park, West Sussex 127, 129, *129*, *177*
   Carved Room 127, *127*
   Grand Staircase *127*
Pevsner, Nikolas *109*, *124*
Pike of Stickle, Lake District *19*
Plant, Tony *59*
Potter, Beatrix 21, 115
   The Tale of Peter Rabbit 47, 115, *115*
Profumo Affair 67
Puttrell, James W. *26*

Quarrymen, the 155
Quilley, Geoff 48

Rackham, Oliver *168*
Rainham Hall, Rainham, Essex 67
Rainham Marshes, Essex 57
Ramsgate, Kent 271, 275
Ransome, Arthur 21
Ravenglass, Cumbria 239, *243*
Ravenscar, North Yorkshire *262*
Rawnsley, Canon Hardwicke *204*
Rawnsley, Rosalind: *Entrust 204*
Read, Simon 286, 288–289
   The Humber Estuary from South Ferriby to Burton Stather 288, 289
Reading, Berkshire 57
Red Earth
   River (from 'Chalk' project) *61*
   Trace (from 'Geograph' project) *60*
Repton, Edward 139
Repton, Humphry 129, 130, *133*, 134–135, *134*, 137, 147, 192, 267, 268, 269
   Fragments on the Theory and Practice of Landscape Gardening 139, 147
   Red Book for Sheringham 130, *130*, *131*, *268*, *270*
   Red Books 130
Repton, William 130
Rhaeadr Ddu waterfall, Snowdonia, Wales *237*
Rhossili Bay, Gower Peninsula, Wales *261*
Rigby, Eleanor 155
Ripon, 1st Marquess and Marchioness of 99
Ripon, Marquess of 103
Roberts, Piercy *264*
Roberts, Simon 12, 14, 15, *39*, *73*, *129*, *137*, *209*, *241*, *267*, *299*
"Robin Hood" 174, 176, 183
Robin Hood's Bay, North Yorkshire *262*
Robinson in Ruins (film) 56–57, *56*, 68, 69
Robinson in Space (film) 57
Rocket Post Field, Robin Hood's Bay, North Yorkshire *262*
Rockford Common, New Forest, Hampshire *230*
Rodgers, Chris: *Contested Common Land 237*
Roesel's bush cricket *187*
Romney, George *171*
Rosedene, Worcestershire *157*
Royal Academy, London 22
Royal Horticultural Society 195
'Rule Britannia' *264*
Runnymede, Old Windsor, Surrey *231*

Sackville-West, Vita 45, *225*
St Mary's Priory, opposite Runnymede *180*, 181
St Michael's Tower, Glastonbury Tor, Somerset *75*
St Peter's church, Stourton, Wiltshire 65, *65*, *107*
Salisbury Plain, Wiltshire 71
Scafell Pike, Cumbria 15, 25, *25*, 26, 27, *31*, 239
Scafell Pike Trail *25*
Scott, William Bell
   Building the Roman Wall 85–86, *86*
   Iron and Coal 86, 89, *89*
Seaton Delaval Hall, Northumberland 117–118, *117*, *118*
Sebald, W.G.: *The Rings of Saturn* 279
Segedunum Roman Fort, Hadrian's Wall 89
Seine River 56
Seven Sisters cliff range *256*
Severnside Hills *150*
Shakespeare, William
   birthplace, Stratford-upon-Avon, Warwickshire 29, 174
   As You Like It 171
   King Lear 256
   A Midsummer Night's Dream 99
Sharington, Sir William *104*
Shaw, George Bernard 47
Shaw's Corner, Ayot St Lawrence, Hertfordshire *47*
Sheerness, Kent 57
Sheffield, Yorkshire *167*, *251*
Sheffield Park, East Sussex *197*
Shell Bay, Dorset *297*
Sheringham, Norfolk 12, 135, 137, 268, 269, 270, *270*
Sheringham Park, Norfolk 15, 130, *130*, *134*, 135, *135*, 137, *137*, 139, 192, 194, 267, 269, *271*
Sheringham Hall 130, *133*, 135, 267, *269*
   Temple 267, 268–269, *268*, *269*
Sherwood Forest, Nottinghamshire 174, 176, *225*
Shipsides, Dan
   Radical Architecture exhibition *26*
   Zig Zag (Puttrell c.1900) 26, 27
Shirley, Sir Robert *109*
Shoeburyness, Essex 277, 279
Silbury Hill, Wiltshire 69, 76
Sinclair, Iain 56
Sissinghurst Castle, Kent 45, *144*, 165, *225*
Skell River *101*, *125*
Slindon, South Downs, West Sussex *220*
Smith, Walter Parry Haskett *27*
Smith, William (Melbourne joiner) *109*
Soane, Sir John *227*
Solway River 83
Somerset 73, 290
Somerset Levels *75*
South Downs *61*, 213, *213*, *214*, *251*
South Milton Sands, Devon *296*
South Seas 49
South West Coast path 290
Southend-on-Sea, Essex 277
Southwell Minster, Nottinghamshire 141
Southwell workhouse, Nottinghamshire 139, *139*, *140*, 141, *141*
Spalding, Lincolnshire 99
Speckled Wood, Swan Barn Farm, Haslemere, Surrey 185, *185*
Stackpole Quay, Pembrokeshire, Wales *263*
Staunton Harold, Leicestershire 102, *109*
Stephenson, George 86
Stonehenge, Wiltshire 15, 71, *71*, 73, *73*, 75
Stonethwaite valley, Cumbria *8*
Stoneywell, Leicestershire *157*

Stour River 34, 35–36, *37*
Stourhead, Wiltshire 65, *65*, 73, *107*, *123*
   Palladian Bridge *65*
   Temple of Apollo *67*
Stowe, Buckinghamshire
   Oxford Bridge *123*
   Temple of Friendship *93*
Straw, Walter 147, *147*, 148–149, *148*
Straw, William 147
Straw, William, Jnr 147–148, *147*, 149
Strawberry Field Salvation Army children's home, Woolton, Liverpool 155
Stubbs, George 40
Studland Beach, Dorset *297*
   Middle Beach *12*
Studley Royal Water Garden, Ripon, North Yorkshire *125*
   St Mary's church 99, *103*
Suffolk 35, 289
Sunnycroft, Wellington, Shropshire *113*, *115*
Surrey Hills *47*
Sustead, Norfolk 130
Sutton Hoo, Suffolk *81*
Swan Barn Farm, Haslemere, Surrey 185, *185*, 186, *186*, *187*
Symonds, Reverend H.H. 239

Tahiti, South Pacific 50, *50*
Takeley Hill, Hatfield Forest, Essex *173*
Talbot, John Ivory *103*
Talbot, Matilda *119*
Tamar River *4*
Tattershall Castle, Lincolnshire: 'House of Bling' exhibition *61*
Teeside 207
Thames Estuary 57, 277
Thames River 19, 54, 56, *57*, 68, 180, *180*, *182*, 273
Thames Valley 56
Thornham, Norfolk 244
Three Cliffs Bay, Gower Peninsula, South Wales *4*
Thurlestone Rock, off South Milton Sands, Devon *296*
Tillemans, Peter 231, 233
Tolpuddle Tree, Dorset 180
Trafalgar, Battle of (1805) 267
Trelissick Garden, Cornwall *191*
Trengwainton, Cornwall: Lower Stream Garden *201*
Trent Falls 289
Trent River 285, 287, 289
Trewavas Cliff, Cornwall *265*
Tucker, James Walker: *Hiking 20*
Turner, J.M.W. 22, 25, 56, 127, *127*, 129, 273, 275
   Morning Amongst the Coniston Fells, Cumberland 22, *23*
   The New Moon, or 'I've Lost My Boat, You Shan't Have Your Hoop' 273
   Stonehenge during a Storm 71
Tyne River 83, 89
Tyneham, Dorset 118
Tyneside 86, 89, *89*

Uffington Castle, Oxfordshire *75*
Ullswater, Cumbria *169*
UNESCO World Heritage Convention 8
Upcher, Abbot 130, *130*, 135, 267, 268–269
Upcher, Charlotte 130, *130*, 135, 267
Upcher family 137, 269
Upper Conwy, Wales *249*

Vanbrugh, John 117
Vaughan Williams, Ralph *47*
Vaughan-Thomas, Wynford *168*
Veitch, John *197*
Veitch Nurseries *197*

Wallington Hall, Northumberland 85, 86, *86*, 89
Wallsend, Hadrian's Wall 89
Wanstead, London 187
War Office 213
Ward, John: 'Come Sable Night' 283
Wasdale, Scafell, Cumbria *25*, *31*
Wasdale Head, Cumbria *241*
Wastwater, Wasdale, Cumbria *14*, 15, *25*, *31*, 239, *239*
Watendlath, near Derwentwater *19*
Watkins, Alfred 76
Watson-Watt, Sir Robert *280*
Weald, the 174, 194
Wedgwood family *47*
Wembury Point, near Plymouth, Devon *263*
Wenlock Edge, Shropshire *167*
Wessex *43*, 73, 75
West Country 75
West Kennet Long Barrow, Wiltshire 69
Weybourne chalk cliffs, Norfolk *271*
Weybourne Windmill, Norfolk *135*
Wharfedale, Yorkshire *213*
Wheal Trewavas copper mine, Cornwall *265*
Whin Sill, Northumberland *83*, 84, *85*
White Cliffs of Dover, Kent 12, 255–256, *255*
White Horse, Uffington, Oxfordshire *75*
White Lady Falls, Devon *169*
White Park Bay, Co. Antrim *79*
Whiteford Burrows and Sands, Gower Peninsula, Wales *261*
Wicken Fen nature reserve, Cambridgeshire *249*
Wicken Vision 249
Wild Ennerdale Partnership *250*
Wilhelm II, Kaiser *199*
Willingale, Tom 187
Willington, Bedfordshire: Dovecote *225*
Willy Lott's House, East Bergholt, Suffolk *35*, *39*
Wilson, Louise K.: *A Record of Fear* 283
Wiltshire 73, *75*
Wimbledon Common, south-west London 244
Wimpole Estate, Cambridgeshire *227*
Wimpole Hall, Cambridgeshire *95*
Winkworth Arboretum, Godalming, Surrey 194, *195*
   Rowe's Flashe Lake *193*
Woburn, Bedfordshire 192
Woodstock Manor, Oxfordshire 117
Woolf, Leonard and Virginia *11*, *43*
Woolsthorpe Manor, Lincolnshire 180
Woolton village church, Liverpool 155
Wootton Bassett, Wiltshire 283
Wordsworth, Dorothy 28
Wordsworth, William 9, 15, 21, 27, 28, *28*, 29, *29*, 35, 39, 42, 55, 56, 169
   The Fraternal Four 179
   Guide to the Lakes 29, 203
   Upon Westminster Bridge 55
Wordsworth Country 29
Worksop, Nottinghamshire 147, 148, 149

Yorkshire Dales *237*
Ysbyty Estate, Wybrant Valley, Gwynedd *249*
Ysbyty Ifan, Wybrant Valley, Gwynedd *249*